Following In Their Footsteps

Rocky Mountain Climbers Club hiked to Arapaho Glacier in 1920.

Following In Their Footsteps

Historical Hikes of the Northern Front Range

Kay Turnbaugh
with Lee Tillotson

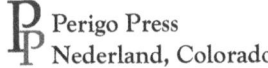
Perigo Press
Nederland, Colorado

Copyright ©2019 Kay Turnbaugh and Lee Tillotson

ALL RIGHTS RESERVED. No part of this book may be reproduced without written permission from the publisher, except in the case of brief excerpts in critical reviews and articles. Address all inquiries to: Perigo Press, PO Box 931, Nederland, Colorado 80466.

ISBN: 978-0-9702532-7-9

SAFETY NOTICE: Although Perigo Press and the authors have made every attempt to ensure that the information in this book is accurate at press time, they are not responsible for any loss, damage, injury, or inconvenience that may occur to anyone while using this book. You are responsible for your own safety and health while hiking. The fact that a trail is described in this book does not mean that it will be safe for you. Be aware that trail conditions change from day to day. Always check local conditions and know your own limitations.

Also by Kay Turnbaugh and Lee Tillotson:
Rocky Mountain National Park Dining Room Girl, The Summer of 1926 at the Horseshoe Inn

Also by Kay Turnbaugh:
Images of America: Around Nederland
The Last Wild West Cowgirl: A True Story
The Mountain Pine Beetle—Tiny but Mighty
Afoot & Afield: Denver, Boulder, Fort Collins, and Rocky Mountain National Park (with Alan Apt)

Front and back cover photos courtesy Rocky Mountain Climbers Club
Cover design: Kay Turnbaugh and Bill Ikler
Book design: Kay Turnbaugh

*This book is dedicated
to all those who have come before
and left us clues to follow in their footsteps.*

Overview map of hike locations

1- Fall River Road
2- Rock Creek Ski Area
3- Mont Alto
4- Arapaho Pass
5- Corona and Rollins Pass
6- Caribou
7- Lost Lake
8- Chautauqua

CONTENTS

- 1   Fall River Road and Milner Pass
- 17   Rock Creek Ski Area and the Winter Olympics
- 35   Mont Alto and The Switzerland Trail
- 51   Arapaho Pass and the Glacier Route
- 69   Corona and Rollins Pass
- 91   Caribou: Wind and Wealth
- 107   Lost Lake
- 119   Chautauqua

Acknowledgements...142
Photo Credits...143
Map Credits...144
Bibliography...145
Index...147

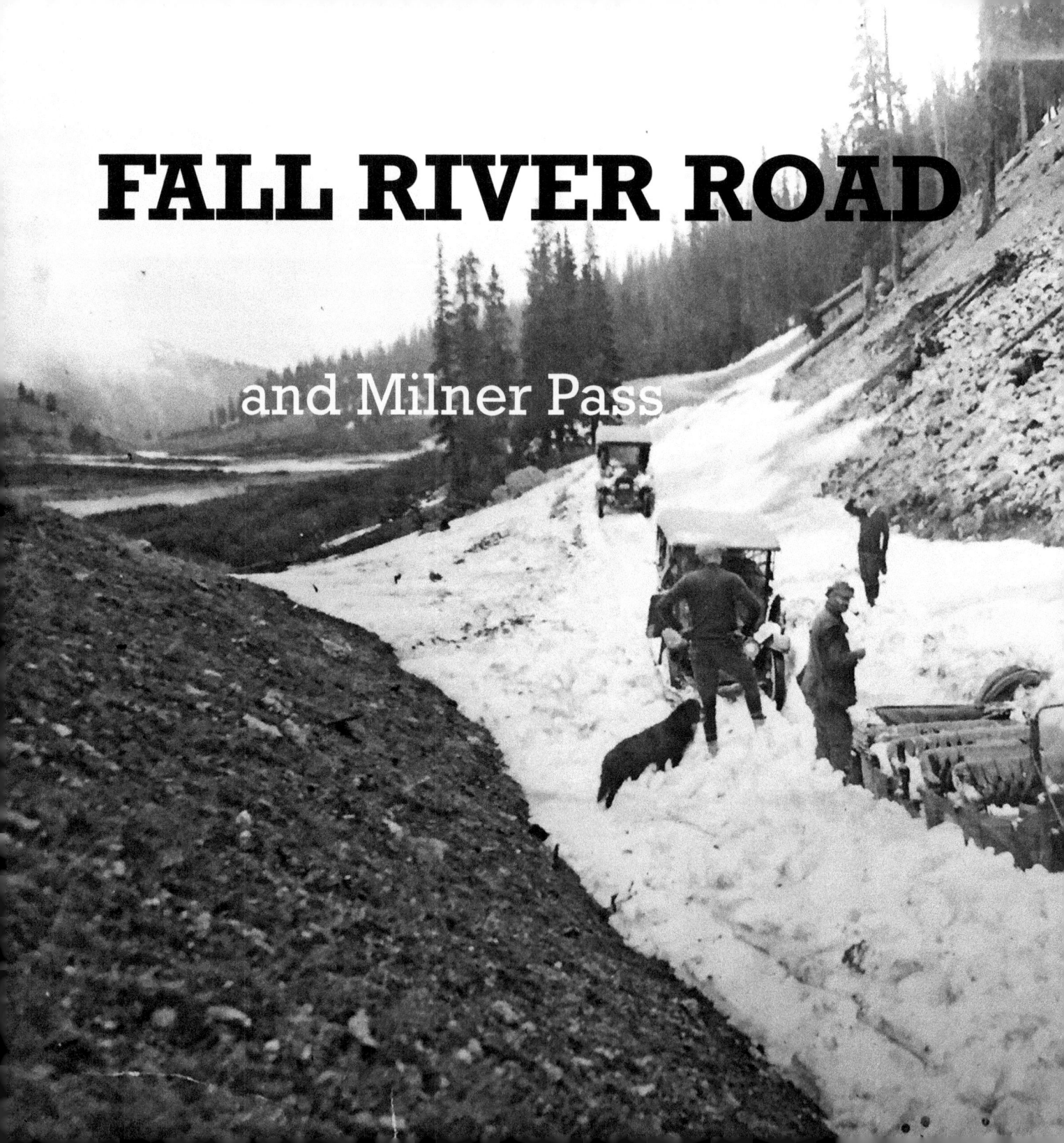

FALL RIVER ROAD
and Milner Pass

THEN AND NOW— Getting stuck in deep snow was common-place on the old Fall River Road. Drivers of a White Bus and two passenger cars consulted about the problem at Poudre Lake in 1923. The lake can be seen in the background. Above: The same site in summer today.

Linking east and west

Before Trail Ridge Road there was Fall River Road—and both of them were preceded by a pack-trail that Native Americans used to cross the Continental Divide.

The Arapahos called Fall River Trail the Dog's Trail because snow that often stayed on the trail until late summer enabled their dogs to pull travois. The trail was marked

THEN AND NOW
Above: Forest Canyon Trail met Fall River Road at the head of Forest Canyon. The sign reads, "Trail Ridge Trail/ Estes Park 20 mi."
Right: Today, the summit of Forest Canyon Pass is marked by a sign that denotes the elevation as 11,320 feet.

Tourists soaked in the expansive view of Fall River Canyon and road from Fall River Pass.

with stone cairns, and the present Ute Trail in Rocky Mountain National Park partially follows the ancient route.

When white hunters and trappers began using the Native American route, they improved it somewhat for horse travel. Early residents of Grand Lake and Estes Park used the trail to connect with each other, and business owners began to see the value in a road that would connect the two tourist centers. They hoped a road over the mountains would draw tourists to drive a scenic circle loop from Denver, through the area that would soon be Rocky Mountain National Park, and back to Denver over Berthoud Pass, crossing the Continental Divide twice on a 225-mile trip.

Construction of the road began simultaneously on both sides in September 1913. Funding was a problem in the beginning, and creative ways to build it were explored. To start construction, thirty-eight convicts from the Colorado State Penitentiary in Cañon City, called

SWITCH BACK ON ESTES PARK GRAND LAKE ROAD

Top: A treacherous, narrow road with numerous switchbacks and steep grades, Fall River Road nonetheless was hugely popular, used by 500 cars a day during the summer of 1926. Bottom: Tour buses had to wait in line at the top of the switchbacks for their turn at descending the hairpins that revealed new vistas at every turn.

"Tom Tynan's boys" after warden Thomas Tynan, were housed in cabins and tents in upper Horseshoe Park and began work in late summer of 1913.

Working only with hand tools, shovels, picks, and augers, construction was painfully slow. Clearing was done with axes and saws, and grubbing (pulling stumps) with horses or mules. Horse teams pulling scrapers and drags were used for some work. Explosives, probably blasting powder, required much difficult drilling before charges could be placed. In the later years of construction, some early tractors and stream shovels were brought in to help with the work of clearing out the rubble left from dynamiting.

Fall River Road was the first road built to take visitors into the interior of the proposed national park, and even though by the end of the 1914 season the work crew had completed only a mile of road, that didn't stop tourists from driving as far as they could, although they

After Trail Ridge Road opened, the western half of Fall River Road was closed to motor traffic and the east side was maintained for one-way traffic only.

A crowd gathered in 1912 for the start of construction on Fall River Road two miles above Chasm Falls.

were advised not to talk to the convicts because it would slow their work.

When Rocky Mountain National Park was formally established in 1915, the road extended only about two miles into the park, and Acting Park Supervisor C.R. Trowbridge reported that the twelve-percent grade above Chasm Falls on the east side of Fall River Road had a switchback so narrow that vehicles had to make a "see-saw" maneuver to complete the turn. There was no wall or railing to prevent a car from going over the cliff. Trowbridge recommended that work be stopped until a survey could be completed for the rest of the route. In the meantime, because he lacked additional funds, Trowbridge contracted only to have the second switchback widened at a cost of $181.40.

After two years of work, the convict crew was replaced by contractors hired by Larimer County on the east side and by Grand County on the west. Construction on the west side followed the old Lulu City wagon road, and the plan was that the two roads would meet in the middle.

On Sept. 14, 1920, contractor Dick McQueary and Park Superintendent L.C. Way drove their vehicles over the road from Grand Lake to Estes Park. A week and a half later, the road was formally opened to public travel.

According to a postcard of Indian Profile Rock, "*Legends of the Utes tell of good fortune showered upon tribesmen who worshipped at this nature-carved likeness of their famous war chief, Arrowhead. Many modern tourists crossing Fall River Pass…pause to experiment with the efficacy of the legendary Indian magic.*" Indian Profile Rock is no longer visible from the road.

A color postcard showcased a car and tourists on Fall River Road.

Seven long years after construction began, Fall River Road was open, and the Park Service began actively promoting it. Soon it was packed with bumper-to-bumper cars and buses, and the two-way traffic made negotiating the steep, narrow dirt road even more treacherous.

A drive over the Continental Divide on Fall River Road was quite an adventure with sixteen switchbacks and a grade that reached sixteen percent in some places. The road was generally well built, although some stretches were only eight to ten feet wide. Often, cars were reduced to backing up the steeper grades because their gravity-feed fuel systems and low gear ratios meant they had more power in reverse. Still, more than 30,000 vehicles traveled Fall River Road in its first full season.

In just a few years, it was clear that Fall River Road had to be replaced. It was being loved to death in spite of how narrow and dangerous it was, and maintenance was a constant battle.

A replacement road that wound even higher across the tundra than Fall River Road was planned. The road would be wider and paved, and its curves easier to negotiate. Work began on Trail Ridge Road in September 1929, and it was completed to Fall River Pass three years later, in July 1932. The maximum grade on Trail Ridge Road is seven percent, far easier to navigate than the sixteen-percent grades on the old Fall River Road.

After Trail Ridge Road was completed, some of the western section of Fall River Road was abandoned and partially obliterated, and a hiking trail was established along parts of it. The eastern section is still in use today as a one-way uphill scenic drive.

For those who travel the old road by foot, it still yields the spectacular views that made it so popular from the day it opened. If you start above treeline near the Alpine Visitors Center, the trail gently descends to Milner Pass, past lakes and through forests steeped in the history of a long-used Contintental Divide crossing.

THEN AND NOW—Early tourists stopped on Fall River Road to view the Poudre Lake spires and the lake below. Their car is parked at one of the three points where the road crosses the Continental Divide. Today, hikers can access the spires from the the trail above the lake.

No stockades, no ball and chain

Thomas Tynan

Prison labor for highway construction was used in Colorado starting in 1900, but it wasn't until 1909, when Thomas J. Tynan was appointed to the office of warden, that the program took on significance. He made groundbreaking changes in the way prisoners were treated, and under his administration it was possible for every man who was willing to work to have employment. Unguarded prisoners worked outside the prison and stayed in camps.

"Instead of sending broken revengeful men back into the world—in no wise reformed but simply trained to greater cunning—there are being restored mended men eager and willing to be made as such use as society will permit," Tynan wrote.

A newspaper reported: *"Fifteen life-termers are among the 300 convicts who in khaki-clad gangs of about sixty are blasting out good roads through the Rockies. They work under unarmed overseers, with no stockades, no barbed wire, no ball and chain, no growl of guns. Nine o'clock at night sees a roll-call at each road camp. Then the gang climbs into its tented bunks and the camp's solitary rifle is shouldered by the night guard-convict, who keeps a keen lookout for coyotes. Less than one-half of one per cent of the convicts so trusted have escaped since Colorado's first road camp was pitched, May 12, 1908."*

Thirty-eight convicts from the Colorado State Penitentiary in Cañon City were brought in to work on building Fall River Road. They were housed in cabins and tents in upper Horseshoe Park and began work in late summer of 1913. Working only with hand tools, they completed two miles in two years.

Maintenance: A formidable task

A cloudburst on July 23, 1923, eradicated five miles of road and stranded one bus and five passenger cars. Above: Rockfalls were common on the road. In July 1936, these workers moved rock from old Fall River Road.

Fall River Road proved to be a maintenance nightmare. As soon as it opened, park crews started filling mudholes and improvement work began. Some switchback curves were widened as soon as possible to permit large busses to pass each other without reversing.

Entire sections of the road often were wiped out by rockslides and floods. A cloudburst on July 23, 1923, eradicated five miles of road and stranded one bus and five passenger cars.

Clearing the road each spring was a herculean effort. Snow depth could exceed 40 feet. Near the upper part of the road, a large drift called Old Faithful often covered the 16-foot telegraph poles that ran along the road. The snowdrift could be 1,200 feet long and 25 feet high. In June of 1929 the Old Faithful drift avalanched every day between and 2 and 3 p.m. for 13 consecutive days.

The Estes Park Trail newspaper described snow removal operations in 1924. *"This road is cleared principally with hand labor. Shovel gangs make a trench through the drifts half a dozen feet wide, leaving the bottom thirty inches of snow to protect the road from washing during subsequent melting. Horses in harness are then driven through the passageway until they become accustomed to the footing. Then a four-horse team draws*

a light wagon through. Within a few days melting has usually made it possible to go through with a wagon of supplies for workers farther up the pass...

"Conditions under which the men work are most severe. Rubber boots and dark glasses are provided for them, but camp conditions are poor. The clothing of the workers gets wet every day and because of the lack of fuel and continuing storms great difficulty is experienced in drying it at night. Many of the men work day after day in wet garments...Winds are terrific, tearing the tents in which the crew eat and sleep and they have to be firmly anchored to prevent them from blowing away entirely.

"Some workers became snow blind after working a single day without sunglasses. Many of the

Above: Shovel gangs started by making a trench and then widening it to open Fall River Road for the summer tourist season. Right: Dynamite was used where the drifts were deepest to start the process of clearing the road.

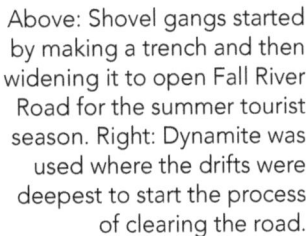

men smeared their faces with grease paint or charcoal, and some wore dark veils, but even these precautions sometimes did not prevent them from suffering badly blistered faces."

The park administration had trouble keeping men at work under such conditions, and Superintendent Roger Toll had two stone shelters built for the crews that worked on maintaining the road. One of them is still standing next to the Alpine Visitors Center.

The problem of clearing snow in the spring was so severe that superintendent Toll suggested using dynamite to clear the road, and in October 1924, after the road was closed to automobile traffic, 13 boxes of dynamite weighing 650 pounts were placed at the point of the deepest drift. The boxes were connected by a special type of hollow lead fuse, filled with TNT, which would explode them all simultaneously.

On June 1, the public was invited to witness the explosions when the charges were set off, and a steam shovel was brought in to help the men with shovels remove the 1,000 cubic yards of snow. Often, the first few automobiles had to be pulled through by horses. That year the road opened to tourist travel on June 13, six days earlier than ever before.

SEASON OPENER—The first passenger bus was hauled over Fall River Road by a team of horses on June 20, 1923.

15647. Water to the Atlantic—Water to the Pacific
Milner Pass, Fall River Road
Rocky Mountain National Park

Fall River Pass tops out at 11,796 feet, but it does not cross the Continental Divide. Milner Pass, over 1,000 feet lower in altitude, does. As this postcard proclaims, "Water to the Atlantic—Water to the Pacific." From the top of Milner Pass a little stream starts its trip to the Mississippi River, and Beaver Creek flows west to the Colorado River. The pass was named in honor of T.J. Milner, who was prominent in railroad circles in Colorado. He was city engineer for Leadville, one of the oganizers of the Denver and Salt Lake Western Railroad Company, and he designed a road to run from Denver to Fort Collins. He was chief engineer of the Denver Tramway Company and surveyed a railroad route to cross the mountains at Devils Thumb Pass, but this scheme of David Moffat's was abandoned.

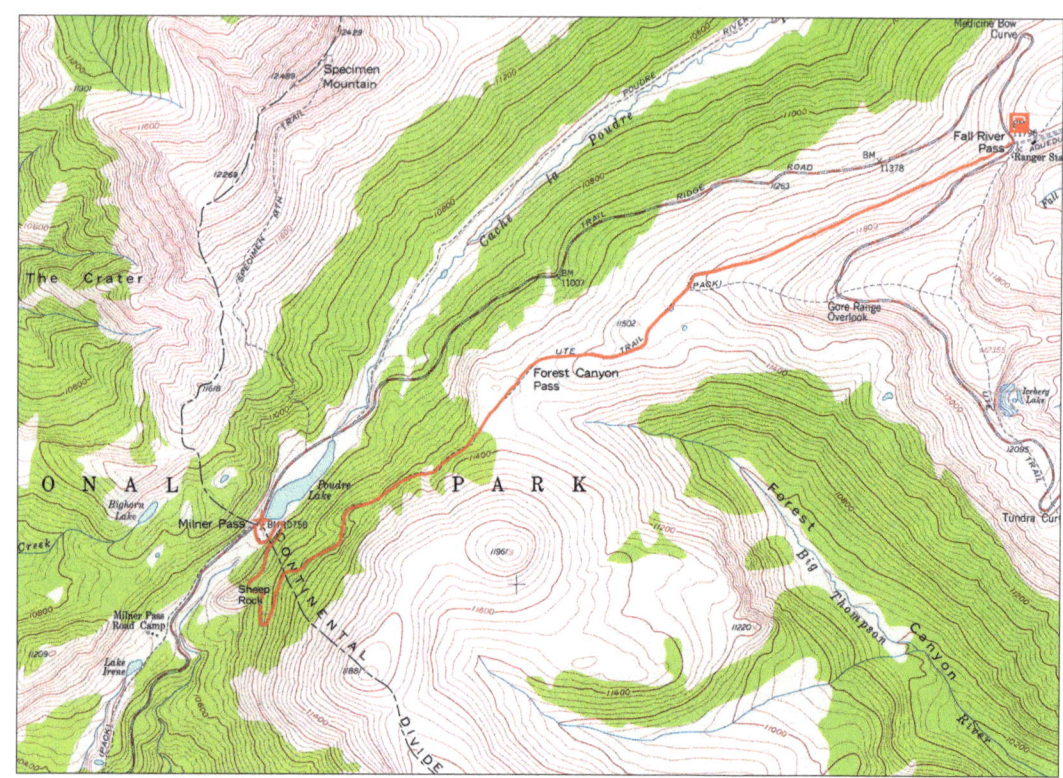

Left: The old Fall River Road hike on a 1958 USGS map. Below: The route on a 1921 map.

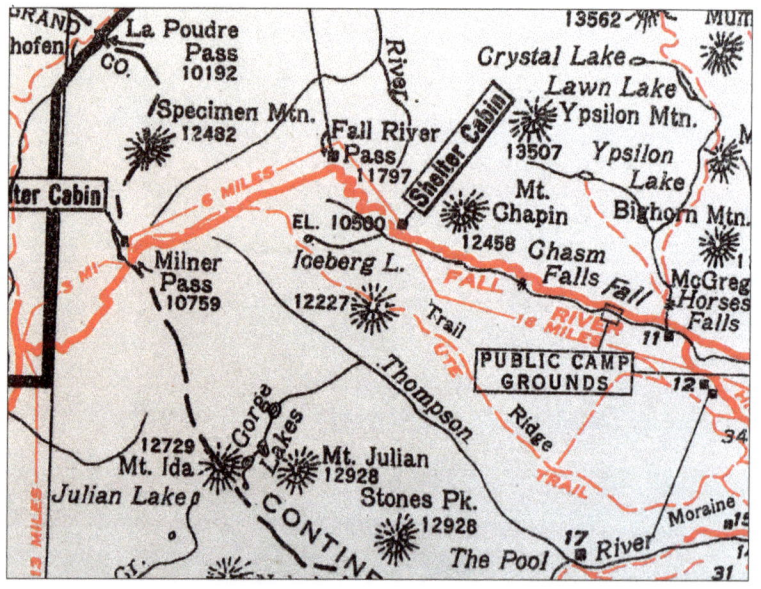

Museums/Side Trips

✯ Estes Park Museum, www.colorado.gov, click on Estes Park Museum

✯ MacGregor Ranch Museum, www.macgregorranch.org

✯ Estes Park YMCA Dorsey Museum, www.ymcarockies.org

✯ Grand Lake Lodge and Town of Grand Lake, www.grandlakehistory.org, www.grandcountyhistory.org

You can hike the old Fall River Road bed from the Alpine Visitors Center down to Milner Pass.

The trail today

For an almost entirely downhill hike, leave a car at Milner Pass or find someone who will drop you off at the Alpine Visitors Center and meet you at the Milner Pass parking area. A little over 6 miles, the hike takes about 2.5 hours. The views are never-ending, including a series of ponds around Forest Canyon Pass and the peaks of the Continental Divide and the Never Summer Range in the distance. Lightning can be a factor whenever you're above treeline, so start early in the day to avoid afternoon thunderstorms. The hike ends almost 1,000 feet lower than the Visitors Center at Poudre Lake and Milner Pass, just below the photogenic rock spires.

ROCK CREEK SKI AREA
and the Winter Olympics

THEN AND NOW— A lone skier crossed one of the ski runs before Rock Creek Ski Area opened on an early morning in 1948. Above: Solitary tracks today cross where once there were many.

Hold on! A rope towed skiers uphill

Skiing up the quiet Rock Creek valley today, it's hard to imagine that it once was home to five ski jumps and a bustling ski area.

Skiing in Allenspark has a long history. One of the town's founding fathers, "Big Jim" Scobee, made a pair of skis from four-inch flooring boards. Soon many Allenspark people were skiing around on their own

THEN AND NOW— The skier facing to the right (opposite page, center right) was hanging onto the rope tow for a ride uphill in February 1949. Opposite page, bottom: Almost 70 years later a skier stopped for a snack at the bottom of the same hill. Above: The base area was a busy place when Rock Creek ski area was operating.

homemade skis or on Northland skis purchased from the local Park Supply Store. One of the first ski manufacturers, Northland got its start in St. Paul, Minnesota, in 1912. Today, Northland is based in Steamboat Springs.

The Northland representative in Allenspark was Lars Haugen, a native of Norway who emigrated to the U.S. with his brother Anders. During the early 1900s he carried the mail from Ward to Allenspark on skis. Lars thought the Allenspark area could be home to a ski resort, and he built a ski run with help from Hans Hansen, who worked for Carl Howelsen in Steamboat Springs. The Haugen Slide opened in 1918, and it was popular enough by 1922 that Haugen designed the nearby Willow Creek area, which was used primarily for jumping and tournaments. Skiing at an Allenspark ski area at the time consisted mostly of climbing to the top of the slide with your skis over your shoulder and then hurtling down a narrow cut in the trees, flying off the jump and soaring through the air to a slightly wider area for landing.

Spectators (in the background) lined the sides of the jumping course for the Fourth Annual Ski Tournament in Allenspark in 1925, obviously a scant snow year. It was estimated that 600 people came to Allenspark to watch the 1925 competition. In the foreground, competitors lined up for a group photo, showing off the heavy wooden skis they carried to the top of the hill.

During the 1920s and '30s the ski areas of Allenspark collectively belonged to the U.S. Western Ski Association and held sanctioned ski tournaments. A program from 1925 boasted that "some of the world's greatest jumpers, including twin and toboggan jumpers, will appear... See the world's most fascinating sport." Admission was 25 cents, children were free.

Six hundred people braved the winter conditions to watch the jumping contests in Allenspark that year. Participants carried their skis to the top of the course. When they took off, the course officials yelled "Tra-a-ck!" The leather strap bindings that held the skier's boots to the homemade skis often came undone at that point, and when the skier went airborne she had to lean far back to reconnect with her skis as she landed.

In addition to Lars Haugen, several Olympic skiers trained at Allenspark, including Nort Billings, George Hurt, and Bill Hottel, who also was a member of the Tenth Mountain Division, the Camp Hale-trained ski troops of World War II. According to Hottel, the Allenspark skiers found out in the early 1930s that you could turn skis. "They stuck a bunch of poles in the ground at the first big ski area in Colorado at Berthoud Pass and started slalom skiing. Allenspark used the Haugen Slide for a slalom course. They held the slalom on Saturday and Willow Creek for jumping competition on Sunday. There were often 1,500 spectators."

Olympic skier Nort Billings said they used the same skis for everything: for moving around on the snow, for ski jumping, and for cross-country skiing. But most people walked up and slid straight down the course.

A 1,000-foot-long rope tow at Willow Creek was added in 1939. It ran off the rear wheels of a 1926 Dodge. The Allenspark Ski Club was reborn as the Saint Vrain Ski Club and run by Clint Baker, the owner of nearby Fern Cliff Lodge. At the end of World War II, area businesses worked together to help the club develop the Rock Creek Ski Area, hoping it would boost the town's winter revenue.

The Rock Creek Ski Area opened in December 1946 with two rope tows. The main downhill run had a 1,800-foot rope tow powered by a 1946 John Deere "G" engine that carried skiers up the middle of the run. The second tow was powered by the old 1926 Dodge truck engine that had been used on the 1939 jump.

Skiers waited in line for a pull to the top on the rope tow.

Skiers taking a break could sun themselves on the deck of the warming shed in the center of this photo. Below them, skiers lined up to ride the rope tow powered by a 1926 Dodge truck. According to Clint Baker's son Bruce, "One of the biggest headaches the first season of operation was the temperamental nature of the ski tow. It had an infuriating way of breaking down when it was needed most." The rope would come out of the idler wheels or it would break due to overloading and stretching, which would require about an hour to re-splice. In spite of the problems, skiers flocked to the new ski area.

The area had three runs, a 30-meter jump, and a number of open snowfields. A lift ticket cost $1.05 a day. The five cents went to the Colorado Ski Association. Local businesses advertised that you could get a pair of skis, the "new" cable bindings, and poles for about $25.

Boulder County extended a road to the base of Rock Creek Ski Area in 1947. For those who didn't want to drive the new road, a vehicle transported skiers from a parking lot in Allenspark. Lodges in Allenspark offered "ski, eat, stay" packages. For $10 per person per night you could stay at the Bakers' luxury Fern Cliff Lodge in a private room with a bathroom. The more basic Wild Rose Inn offered three-room cottages with cooking facilities for $5 a night.

On a sunny day shortly before the ski area ceased operation, Carol Angevine drank a Pepsi and relaxed on the deck of the Ski Shack. Clara Jane Meier, right, was pulled uphill by the rope tow in 1948.

Above: Philip and Clinton Baker had big plans for a Rock Creek Ski Area expansion. Left: An artist's rendering of their plan.

Rock Creek closed in 1952, a victim of underfunding, temperamental rope tows, and the continual problems of maintaining the three-mile road to the base area. The U.S. Forest Service proposed to revive the ski area in 1958 and issued a prospectus with three new lifts that would have gone up to the summit of Point 10,810 and to the saddle to its east. A third lift would have gone to the southeast shoulder of Saint Vrain Mountain to an elevation of 11,000 feet. The base area would have been moved a half mile up the valley. No one bid on the prospectus, and Rock Creek Ski Area is now only a memory.

With their twin boys on their backs, Gerry and Ann Cunningham tested Gerry's Kiddie Carrier invention at Rock Creek Ski Area. For years, Gerry manufactured his outdoor products in a workshop in his home in Ward, Colorado. He opened Mountain Sports in Boulder and is considered the grandfather of the insulated products business, which includes the nylon and down sleeping bag, clothing, packs, tents, and accessories. In a 15-page booklet that he wrote in 1967 on "How to Keep Warm," Gerry Cunningham penned the now-famous words, "If your feet are cold, put your hat on."

THEN AND NOW—Clint Baker walked through snow that was almost hip-deep at the base of the Rock Creek Ski Area. Today's skiers also revel in the deep powder.

A flyer's breathless experience

Anne Matlack wrote in 1979 about the first time she tried the high jump at Willow Creek in the early 1920s. *"There was a long climb up the irregular frozen footprints at the side of the course. Sometimes I dropped my skis from my shoulder and thrust them through the crust of the snow and I leaned on them, breathing hard and looking back down the course."*

At the top, she pointed her skis downhill, *"thrusting the back halves of them under a scrubby little pine and shelf of rock. Then I stood up, looked over the trees and snow on the hills that I thought I might never see again...I pulled off my mittens and knelt to put my mountain boots, one at a time, into the straps and buckle them, fumbling at them, clamping them slowly. ...I stood up, and my skis began to slip forward of their own accord. I stooped and snatched my mittens and dropped off the rock. The outposts flapped their arms and sent down a long dismal call for 'TRA-A-CK!' Across the wind-swept snow I slid, started toward the trees, and got back into the track just as I shot into the steepest part.*

"I flew down the long white cut in the forest. The trees were just a blur on either side, and I heard the swift murmur above the roar in my ears when I passed the people. I half fell at the holes [left by a previous skier], recovered, touched the [little] bridge [over the gully], and was out toward the field and the trees there.

"THEN I BREATHED. I came to a big pine. My skis went on either side of it. My arms flung 'round it and I stopped with a jerk. The old man who owns the burros stood by and leaned on the handle of his shovel, and he was saying, 'Yessir, you done well.'"

Lars Haugen demonstrated his ski jumping form as he flew off the Haugen Slide.

Looking south from the Ferncliff Lodge, ca. 1948, the view included Turkey Rock and one of the ski runs.

Six courses drew skiers to Allenspark

- Willow Creek,[1] average grade of 18 degrees, 800 feet long
- Thelma Slide, 10 degrees, 318 feet
- Haugen Slide, 19 degrees, 1,830 feet
- Butterbowl or Cooperider Slide,[2] 16 degrees, 400 feet
- Point o' Pines
- Rock Creek Ski Area

Other ski courses: Wildwood Cross Country Course, 3 to 10 degrees, 3 miles; toboggan course, 6 degrees, 1,830 feet

[1]Scaffolding at the top of Willow Creek extended 62 feet above the height of the run, making it possible to watch the jumper's form from the time she flew off the top until she completed the run-out, which was across Willow Creek and up the other side.

[2]The Cooperider was on property owned by the Cooperiders, and people often slid down it in a big butter bowl, which is how it got its second name. When making butter, it was removed from the churn and put in a large wooden bowl to salt and finish before being placed in molds or stored in containers. Those large bowls could also used as sleds.

Skiers carried their skis and walked up the sides of the Tregemba ski run on the ridge just south and west of the original town plat of Allenspark.

The Haugen brothers

The Haugen brothers, Anders (top) and Lars (below), are both in the Colorado Ski Hall of Fame. The Olympic parade coat that Anders wore is on display at the Colorado Snowsports Museum and Hall of Fame in Vail.

Brothers Lars and Anders Haugen immigrated to the United States in 1909 from Telemark, Norway. They had grown up skiing and wanted to introduce the sport to their new countrymen, so they built ski jumps wherever they lived, starting with one for the Milwaukee Ski Club and then in northwestern Wisconsin before heading to Colorado.

The brothers won the U.S. National Championships in jumping 11 times between 1911 and 1920. It was during that time frame that Lars, the older brother, carried the mail on skis between Ward and Allenspark (15 miles each way) and became the Northland skis representative. One of his accounts was the store in Allenspark. Lars built the first ski course in Allenspark, the Haugen Slide.

Anders set successive new world records of 213 feet and 214 feet on the ski jump he built in Dillon, Colorado, in 1919 and 1920. Lars couldn't compete in the 1924 Olympics because he was a professional ski jumper, but Anders, a part-time bricklayer, was the captain of the U.S. ski jumping team at the first modern Winter Olympic Games in Chamonix, France. He placed fourth on the individual large hill, just behind Norway's Thorleif Haug, who had already won three gold medals at the games. Not until 50 years later was a scoring error discovered. Anders had actually won the bronze, America's first Olympic skiing medal. At the age of 86 he traveled to Norway and was given the bronze medal by Anna Maria Magnussen, Haug's youngest daughter. As of 2018, Anders Haugen was the only American to ever have won a medal in ski jumping.

In 1929, Lars and Anders Haugen moved to the Lake Tahoe area, where they remained involved in the development of ski clubs and bringing the joys of skiing to the public. ✺

Norton Billings of Estes Park, Colo., Ski club has been selected as a member of the American Olympic cross-country team, according to word received by his father Wednesday. Billings is now in training at Lake Placid, N. Y., scene of the games early in February. James Harsh of Estes Park also was named on the team.

Homegrown Olympian

Eleven men were sent to Lake Placid to represent the U.S. at the third Winter Olympics in 1932, and three were from Colorado. It was the first time the United States fielded a full ski team at the games.

John Steele, a jumper, was from Steamboat Springs. Jim Harsh of Hot Sulphur Springs and Norton R. Billings of Estes Park were cross country skiers representing the Rocky Mountain National Park Ski Club of Estes Park. Billings was selected to compete in the 50km race, Steele in the jumping event, and Harsh as an alternate in the combined event. Harsh had won the intercollegiate jumping championship in the last three years and was the only man ever to beat Billings in Colorado.

Nort Billings grew up in the mountains around Lyons and was one of the four graduates from Estes Park High School in 1923. His father operated a homestead timbering operation on Fishcreek near Estes Park, and when chores permitted he and some friends learned to cross country ski. They often skied over the Continental Divide from Estes Park to Grand Lake for fun. If he and his siblings were caught by a surprise snowstorm they broke up barrels to use the slats as skis to get to or from school. Nort's first cross country ski race was against a

The sign on the back of the car that took Nort Billings and Jim Harsh to Lake Placid reads, "R.M.N.P. Ski Club, Estes Park, Colo."

bunch of mules that he and his father were driving near Twin Sisters mountain. They turned the animals loose to rest, but instead of resting they suddenly darted up the road at full speed. Nort ran them down and headed them off after a four-mile race on skis.

"He won," said his father.

Nort's first skiing job at age 17 was packing supplies from Estes Park to the winter headquarters of the Colorado Mountain Club at Fern Lake, about five miles each way. He won the Rocky Mountain National Park Ski Club's annual Elkhorn Trophy in 1924, 1925, and 1926. He often competed in Allenspark events, but in 1932 he was 27 years old and married with a small son and hadn't been competing regularly.

With no coaches, Harsh, Steele, and Billings did their own fitness training and competed against other local clubs in Steamboat Springs, Hot Sulphur Springs, and Grand Lake for race experience. Billings consistently outskied Steele and Harsh.

With no official transportation set up for them, Billings and Harsh had to find a way to get to the cross-country trials that were to be held on the Olympic course in Lake Placid, New York. At the time, Olympic competitors had to rely on their own financial resources as there was no corporate or U.S. Olympic Committee support.

Ted Jelsema, an Estes Park friend and secretary of the Estes Park Ski Club, had a "thicker wallet" than the two athletes, as well as a car. He volunteered to drive Harsh and Billings to New York. Estes Park residents took up a collection for the skiers, and they left with $100 for lodging and transportation.

Both Harsh and Billings qualified for the U.S. Olympic team, Harsh as an alternate for both jumping and

Norton Billings, the third Coloradan to be honored with selection on the Olympic team, comes from Estes Park. He has been selected as a cross-country rider. Winter sports enthusiasts in the old home state believe Billings is likely to be the United States' best bet. He has shown the way to fast fields in various tournaments and is set to beat the world and hoist the star-spangled banner on the flagpole.

A two-cent stamp commemorated the Lake Placid Olympics. Billings family lore suggests that Nort Billings was the inspiration for the drawing of the skier.

cross country and Billings for the 50-kilometer (31.07 miles) race.

It was a bad year for snow, and the Olympic course was treacherous. "They took bushel baskets and made a trail about two feet wide, but there just wasn't enough for all the course," Harsh recollected.

"Two-thirds of it was hard-packed icy snow and the other third was willow boughs," Billings said years later in an interview. Even though you could wax for willow branches, he "kept getting tangled up in those branches, and after a while it just wasn't any use…A lot of the kids broke arms and legs at Lake Placid in 1932. The competition was anything but fun." He struggled for five hours and finally had to quit the race when a ski tip splintered. Only about half the field of 39 contestants finished.

Years later a newspaper reporter wrote, "The skis he used during the competition hang in his basement giving mute but ample evidence about the condition of the course. The tip of one is missing. The edges are battered beyond belief."

After the Olympics, Nort Billings returned to Longmont where he owned the Billings Electric Co. and served as City Alderman for several years. He continued to ski and fish in the mountains around Estes Park until his death in 1994. He was inducted into the Colorado Ski Hall of Fame in 1999.

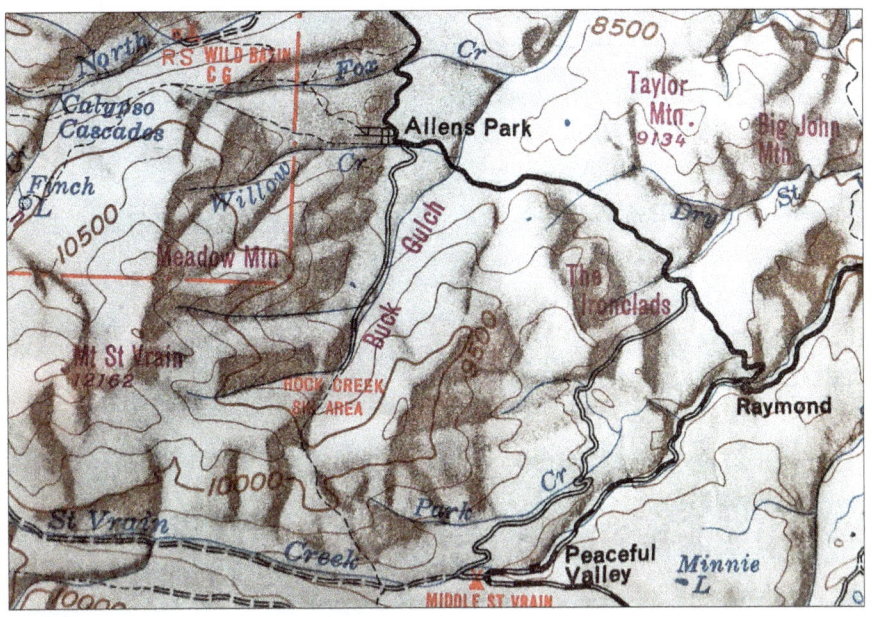

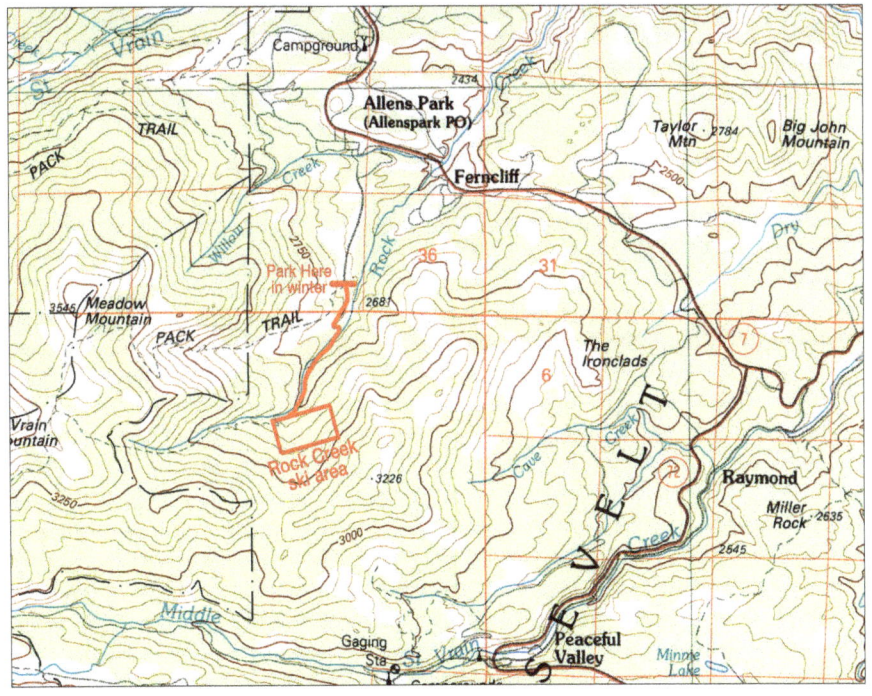

THEN AND NOW—A vintage map (top) shows the location of Rock Creek Ski Area in Buck Gulch. You can find the old ski area off Forest Road 116 on a current map. Opposite page: A hiker climbs up one of the old ski runs at Rock Creek.

The trail today

Turn off the Peak to Peak Highway (CO 7) in Allenspark and drive south on Ski Road. Take a sharp left at 0.1 mile, and then a right after another 0.1 mile. Ski Road (County Road 107) becomes Forest Road 116 at mile 1.3. In another 0.3 mile the road splits. The right fork leads to the Saint Vrain Mountain Trailhead. The left fork goes to the old Rock Creek ski area. In the winter, park at this fork. In the summer, drive as far as you like and walk the road to the old Rock Creek Ski Area site.

Museums/Side Trips

✯ Longmont Museum, www.longmontcolorado.gov

✯ Colorado Ski Museum, Vail, Colorado, www.snowsportsmuseum.org

Mont Alto

and The Switzerland Trail

THEN AND NOW— Longs Peak soared above the Mont Alto pavilion, a popular tourist stop for the Switzerland Trail train route. The structure was moved to Glacier Lake in 1905, and today only the stone chimney and the fountain's ghost remain of the once-vibrant dancing pavilion and lecture hall.

Dancing with wildflowers

Passengers clutched huge bouquets of wildflowers and hung out the windows as the little narrow-gauge train chugged around the last big bend in the tracks before Mont Alto and blew its whistle. They had arrived!

Their day of play in the mountains started that morning when the train puffed out of the Boulder station and headed up the "Whiplash Route," so named for the many twists and turns on its 26-mile route to the "Cloud-Kissed Camp of Ward" at 9,400 feet. To promote the unparalleled moun-

Wildflower excursions, such as this sixth annual one in 1910, made several stops so passengers could get off the train to pick wildflowers, an activity that is illegal today.

tain vistas that unfolded around every bend in the tracks, the Colorado & Northwestern Railroad dubbed the route The Switzerland Trail, noting that it far surpassed anything found in Europe.

The Switzerland Trail offered countless excursions: holiday excursions, moonlight excursions, snowball outings, Sunday School excursions, student excursions, and trips to collect aspen leaves in the fall. Wildflower specials featured stops at selected spots so the fashionably dressed passengers could gather mountain wildflowers. Passengers packed a picnic

lunch, and excursion trains usually pulled a baggage car filled with kegs of beer packed in ice. Passengers paid $1 for a ticket to the mountains and back.

After leaving Boulder, the train's first stop in Fourmile Canyon was Sunset, the location of several booming mines and saloons, a general store and a hotel with a popular dining room. From Sunset, the train turned north toward Gold Hill and Ward and stopped at Mont Alto Picnic Area. Many passengers spent an entire day at Mont Alto—it was a sought-after destination for community picnics, baseball games, dances, concerts, and celebrations of all sorts.

The railroad built a large log dancing pavilion in a grove of "giant ponderosa pines," and visitors could hear lectures from University of Colorado and Chautauqua speakers or just spend time hiking around the extensive grounds, picking wildflowers, and watching for wildlife. Passengers coming to Mont Alto were often greeted by a band, and after disembarking would gather around a spring-fed fountain built with native rocks to soak in the clean mountain air and views that extended west to Longs Peak and east to the plains.

The Whiplash Route

"One need not go to Switzerland for sublime mountain scenery," claimed the C&N Railroad when it opened its Switzerland Trail line. Two other railroad lines had gone bust trying to serve the mining camps in the mountains of Boulder County, but the C&N determined that the railroad could successfully haul ore and supplies—and tourists. So in 1897 it laid tracks past Sunset to Ward to pick up the piles of ore that had been waiting for transportation to the mills below. And it built amenities for sightseers.

The extended line opened in 1898, and the train carried an average of 250 passengers every day, along with its usual loads of ore. Powerful engines were needed to haul the heavy loads up steep grades of 4.39 percent, and three new engines were commissioned from the Brooks Locomotive Works in New York. They were the largest narrow-gauge locomotives in the world at the time.

In 1901 construction began on a line that would turn south from Sunset and run over Sugarloaf Mountain to the gold mining camp of Eldora. The Mont Alto lodge was dismantled and reassembled at Glacier Lake, about two miles southwest of Sunset. The new route opened in 1905.

With the success of the tourist trains, another rail was added that connected to Denver's Union Station so travelers from that city didn't have to change coaches.

Unfortunately, the gold boom in Eldora was short-lived, and several of Ward's big mines shut down after 1905. The railroad's snowplows and the 200 men who sometimes shoveled snow off the tracks were often overwhelmed during the next few winters. Passengers still rode The Switzerland Trail in the summer, but their numbers gradually diminished as motor cars became more popular.

Those factors and a weak economy forced the C&N into bankruptcy in 1909. Optimistic that the excursion specials could support the railroad, the Denver, Boulder, & Western Railroad was formed to succeed the C&N. With the area's mines in decline, the DB&W, nicknamed the "drink beer and wine," decided tourism was the route to success. But Stanley Steamers were taking over the railroad's business. The steam-powered automobile invented by twin brothers Francis and Freelan Stanley was bigger and more powerful than gas-powered vehicles. Stanley Steamers could haul both passengers and freight and hastened the demise of the DB&W. Only tungsten mining during World War I kept the railroad line solvent.

And then floods in 1912 and 1914 in Boulder Canyon damaged wooden trestle bridges and track, necessitating costly repairs. Another flood on July 31, 1919, caused by a cloudburst that dumped 4.8 inches of rain, precipitated the end of the line for The Switzerland Trail of America. The railroad ceased operation in 1920.

Today, portions of the old Switzerland Trail railroad bed can be hiked, biked, or driven. A tall stone chimney and remnants of foundations and the old fountain are all that remain at the original Mont Alto site, along with the spectacular views that have drawn tourists to this historic spot for over a century.

Left: Big hats protected women's faces from the sun, and a band from Longmont welcomed C&N passengers to Mont Alto. The pavilion can be seen in the background, train tracks in the foreground. Below left: Passengers posed on a trestle with the wildflowers they had gathered in August, 1908. Below right: Even in winter women dressed up for a Snowball Excursion ride on The Switzerland Trail.

Decorated with bunting, a festive Engine 30 pulled into Mont Alto with a load of excursionists. Below: a large group of people gathered for a photo in front of the pavilion at Mont Alto. The Mont Alto name was spelled out in white quartz rocks.

The mountains called… and Boulder closed

On a summer Sunday in 1898, a special Switzerland Trail train pulled out of the Boulder station.

The Daily Camera newspaper reported that businesses and banks closed so employees could ride the train to Mont Alto for the formal opening of the "Whiplash Route from the Verdant Valley of Boulder to the Cloud Kissed Camp of Ward." Even the electric light works blew its whistles and closed down at 11:20 so its employees could attend the big celebration of Boulder Day at Mont Alto Park. Two trains headed into the mountains in the morning and one at noon, with three returning at convenient times in the afternoon and evening.

The train wound its way west out of town and up Four Mile Cañon, climbing to Ward where it turned around. But the excursionists weren't going to Ward. They were bound for Mont Alto Park, one of the most popular resorts in Colorado.

Every train was crowded to "utmost capacity." The railroad sold 350 tickets for $1 on Boulder Day. Passengers spent the day picnicking, picking wildflowers, dancing in the pavilion, and drinking the beer that was packed in ice and hauled to the site in a baggage car. The Boulder Band provided music all day and for a dance in the pavilion that night.

The next year an estimated 1,000 people made the trip for Boulder Day. The proceeds of the excursion were used to fund a reception for the returning troops, home from the Spanish-American War.

Excursionists soaked in the views at Point Frankeberger, across from the "Giant's Ladder," the railroad's moniker for track that wound its way up a mountain on a route that looked like the rungs of an enormous ladder. There was another Giant's Ladder between Tolland and Corona on the Moffat Road. Jason Lee Frankeberger planned and laid a system of sewers for Boulder in 1895 and later reconstructed the water system. He was the chief engineer for the building of the Colorado & Northwestern Railroad from Boulder to Ward. His daughter Minette Frankeberger was the first woman to graduate from engineering school at the University of Colorado.

THEN AND NOW—Hikers can see the same views today as they walk the old railroad bed to Mont Alto picnic area.

Four of the passengers on a Switzerland Trail excursion for the Boulder Sanitarium posed for a photograph on the front of Engine 30. The engine was eventually retired to Boulder's Central Park, but vandalism necessitated its move to the Colorado Railroad Museum in Golden.

Engine 30

The Switzerland Trail of America rail line wasn't just for tourists. The original lines were laid to serve the mining industries in Boulder County. Mines in the mountains above Boulder shipped thousands of tons of ore annually to the mills at Boulder and Valmont. On return trips the trains carried loads of mining equipment, supplies, coal, mail, baggage, and other supplies to the mines and towns at a time when serviceable roads and other modes of transportation were almost nonexistent. "In an era of horse-drawn vehicles and almost impossible mountain roads, this was no mean contribution," wrote Dr. J.B. Schoolland of the University of Colorado. Schoolland headed a campaign in 1953 to bring Engine 30 back to Boulder as a memorial to the Switzerland Trail rail line. Engine 30 was one of three specially built for the C&N. Purchased in 1898, it was brought to Boulder on a flat car and unloaded just west of Broadway. At that time it was regarded as one of the most powerful engines in mountain service.

The bad luck railroad

Ernest Greenman, who later became famous for his association with the Rocky Mountain Climbers Club and with the Greenman Drug and Stationery Store on University Hill, was on the survey crew for the new railroad that became The Switzerland Trail. *"We came up Boulder Cañon, then up Four Mile Creek to Sunset, following the general route of the abandoned narrow-gauge Greeley, Salt Lake and Pacific, a branch of the Union Pacific. From Sunset we ran the line over new territory to Ward,"* he told historian Forrest Crossen.

"I helped lay track part of the time and this was completed to Ward May 31, 1898. An engine and a passenger coach made the first trip. ...One Sunday the chief engineer ordered us to survey the site of Mont Alto Park. We ran a line from the spring down to the fountain and laid out the dance hall. The old chimney was in the dance hall.

"The railroad had secured all the mail contracts, which cut out all the stages operating out of Boulder in this territory. Everything went fine until winter shut it down. Snowfall was very heavy and soon there was 30 feet of snow at Camp Francis. The railroad had no rotary snowplow, so they hired 270 men to shovel snow off the tracks. They loaded flatcars with rails, hooked them behind a snowplow and flanger and tried to ram through the drifts that filled the cuts. Finally they had to abandon the road from Puzzler to Ward and send the mail by saddle horse.

"The railroad had bad luck. The mines at Ward, supposed to have great tonnage of low-grade ore, played out...the Eldora line made money only during the construction of the Barker Dam at Nederland, hauling in supplies and machinery. The railroad continued to lose money, so when there was a washout during the summer of 1919 the owners had a good excuse for abandonment."

Engines 30 and 32 "bucked the snow" after a snowslide derailed the tender above the Big Five Mine in 1914.

THEN AND NOW
The abandoned railroad bed of The Switzerland Trail has not changed much in the 120 years since it was built. "The railroad was built by some Pennsylvania capitalists: Blair, Macky, Culbertson and Dick—the Big Four, we called them," remembered railroad surveyor and construction worker Ernest 'Dad' Greenman. "They made a great deal of money with a coal-hauling railroad back there, and they became interested in a railroad to haul ore from the Ward mines to a mill that they built at the Boulder Lakes [Valmont] plant."

THEN AND NOW
Water from a nearby spring was piped to the quartz, red sandstone, and native rock fountain at Mont Alto. It sprayed water into a 20-foot pool. The top of the chimney that still stands today can be seen on the left side of the pavilion and dance hall in the bottom photo.

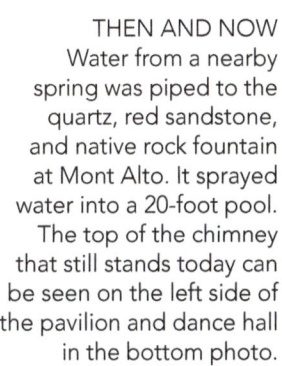

The trail today

From Colorado Highway 72 (the Peak to Peak Scenic Byway) take County Road 52, the Gold Hill Road, east for four miles to County Road 93. It is marked "Switzerland Trail–Mt. Alto Park." Park here and hike the narrow dirt road—the abandoned railroad bed—that goes to the old Mont Alto site. The old chimney from the pavilion still stands and is surrounded by picnic tables and cooking grills. This is an easy 1.2-mile hike with views that live up to The Switzerland Trail of America name.

Museums/Side Trips

★ Colorado Railroad Museum, Golden, Colorado, coloradorailroadmuseum.org (Engine 30 from The Switzerland Trail is located here.)

★ Roadhouse Boulder Depot Restaurant, roadhouseboulderdepot.com

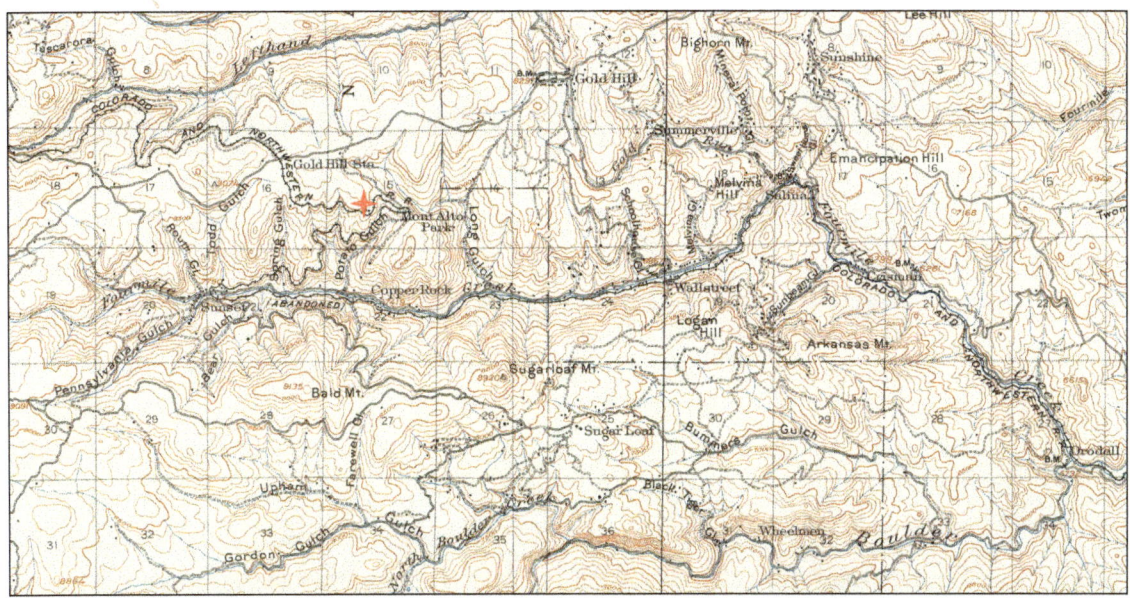

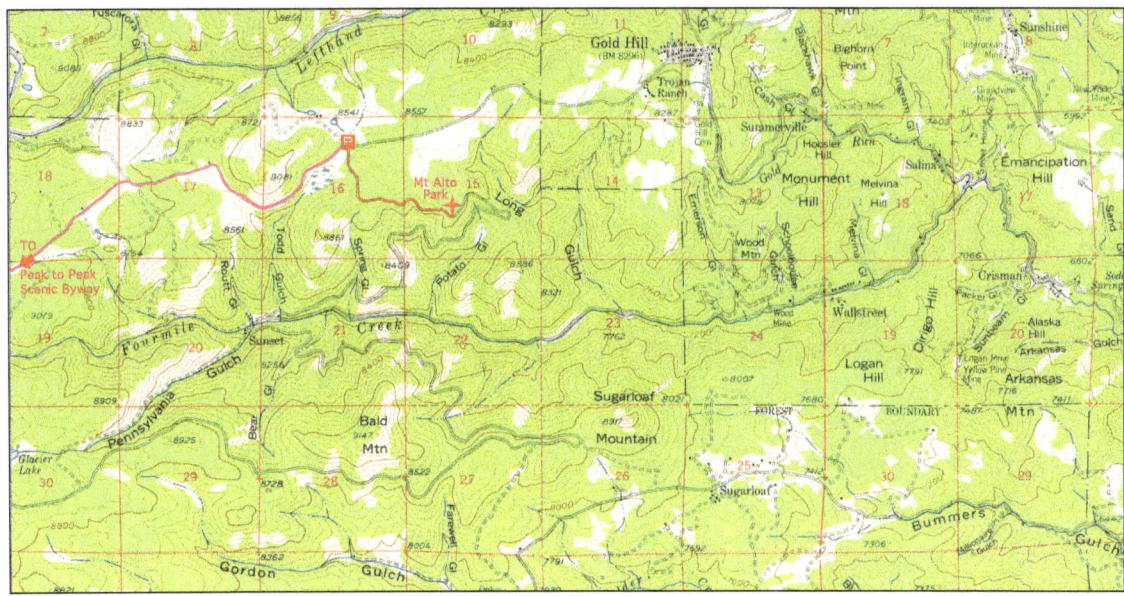

THEN AND NOW
Above: A 1902 map shows the route of the railroad and locates Mont Alto Park a little too far east. Below: The historic hike to Mont Alto is shown in red on the more recent 1957 USGS map.

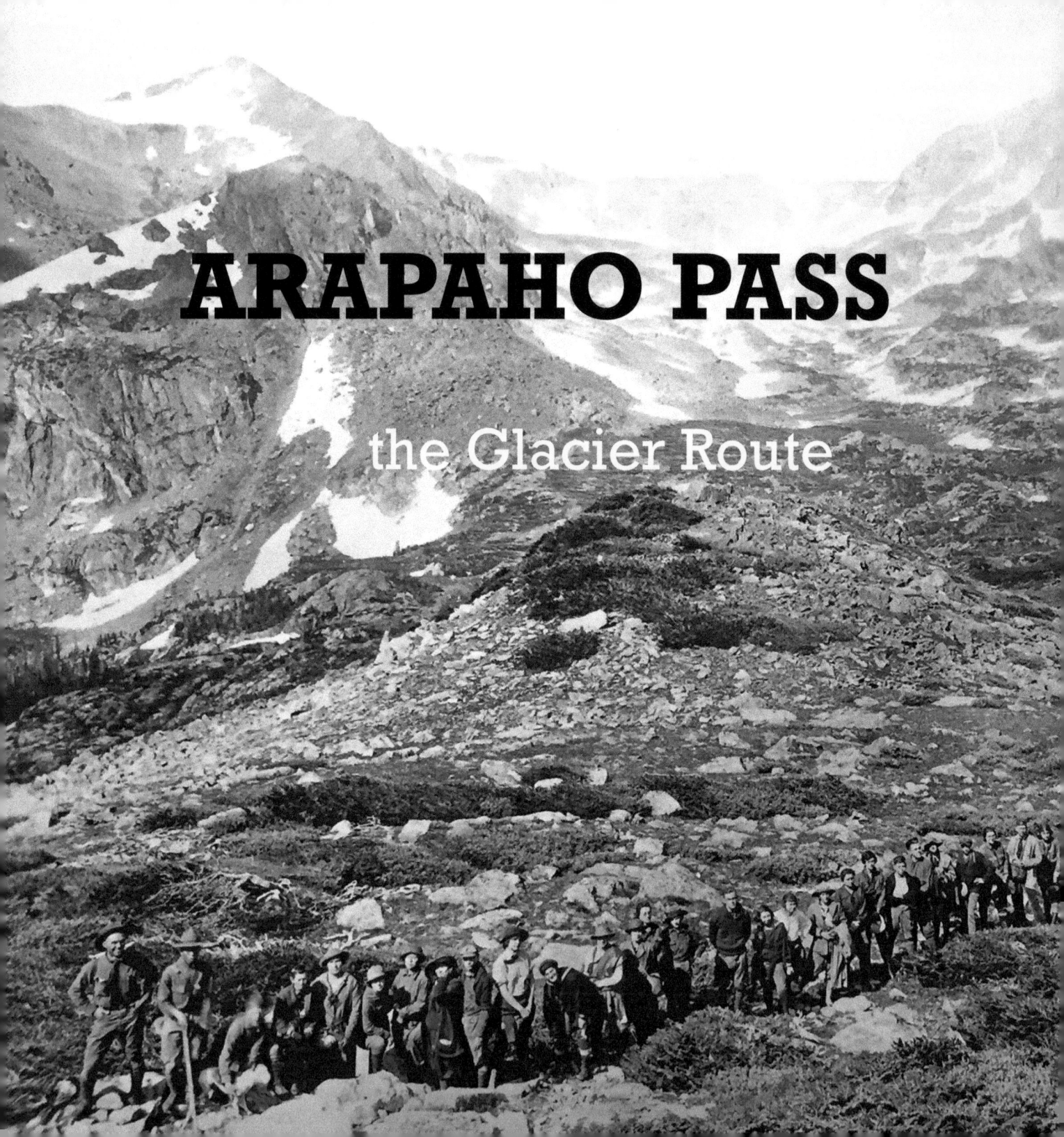

ARAPAHO PASS

the Glacier Route

THEN AND NOW— Rocky Mountain Climbers Club photographer Ed Tangen took this 1921 photo of hikers on the trail to Arapaho Glacier. Today, the trail is as popular as ever.

Boulder's glacier: big business

For 3,000 years people have tramped across the Continental Divide on Arapaho Pass. In the past the route was used to exploit sought-after mineral resources and its namesake glacier. Today it's famous for stunning scenery, wildflowers, and wildlife.

The modern-day glacier tale begins in 1897 when Herbert N. Wheeler of the U.S. Forest Service and his brother-in-law, D.M. Andrews, who owned a nursery in Boulder, hiked across

Eben Fine, top, and Fred Fair, bottom, extolled the wonders of Arapaho Glacier and inspired thousands of people to make the hike every year. Fair named two more of the area's glaciers after himself and his wife Isabelle.

"the big snow bank" below South Arapaho Peak in search of dogtooth violet bulbs. They wrote later that they realized it was "the remnant of a sizeable glacier" that had scoured out a series of lakes which are now a water supply for the city of Boulder. The men reported that the glacier was at least a half mile wide and extended that far from the foot of the peaks.

Soon after, Boulder druggist and chamber of commerce representative Eben G. Fine saw the glacier as an opportunity to bring people to Boulder County. Beginning in 1900, he traveled the country with a lantern slideshow extolling the glacier's scenery. He gave 3,500 lectures, and people began traveling to Boulder to see its glacier. In an effort to attract even more visitors, Enos Mills, naturalist and "Father of Rocky Mountain National Park," wrote a series of articles on the Arapaho Glacier for midwestern newspapers.

Meanwhile, the city of Boulder wanted to bring water from the high mountain streams and glaciers to supply the city. In 1904, Boulder hired Fred Fair as city engineer to design a system to do just that.

Fair began spending more time in the high country as part of his job, and he too became passionate about bringing more tourists to see Arapaho Glacier. He knew that most tourists wouldn't be able or wouldn't want to hike to the glacier, so he proposed building a road—a road that he thought would be more spectacular than the one to the top of Pike's Peak or the road proposed to summit Mount Evans or the one that would become Trail Ridge Road.

Arapaho Glacier was a favorite hike for RMCC members, like this group in 1921. From 1938 to 1974, the Boulder Chamber of Commerce sponsored an annual August hike to Arapaho Glacier. Forty-eight people made the hike in 1938, and by 1974 the annual event had mushroomed to 600 participants. Too many people and heavy environmental damage brought these ultra popular hikes to an end. Arapaho Glacier is now closed to the public.

Boulder began promoting the glacier, and ads appeared in 150 magazines and newspapers across the country. The Colorado legislature was convinced to appropriate $5,000 to turn the Arapaho Pass trail into a road. Instead of following the old trail along the North Fork of Boulder Creek, Boulder County and the U.S. Forest Service planned to build a road through Rainbow Lakes to the southern edge of Arapaho Glacier, continuing it with a figure-eight trail, equipped with hostels, which would cross the Continental Divide at Arapaho, Pawnee, and Buchanan passes.

Following a national publicity campaign for the road, the Forest Service appropriated $56,000 for the road. In 1913

On June 30, 1925, 165 people attended the Chamber of Commerce dedication of the new Rainbow Lakes road. The road was named in honor of James P. Maxwell, a pioneer and a builder of the first road to the Rainbow Lakes region. Fred Fair was the principal speaker at the dedication.

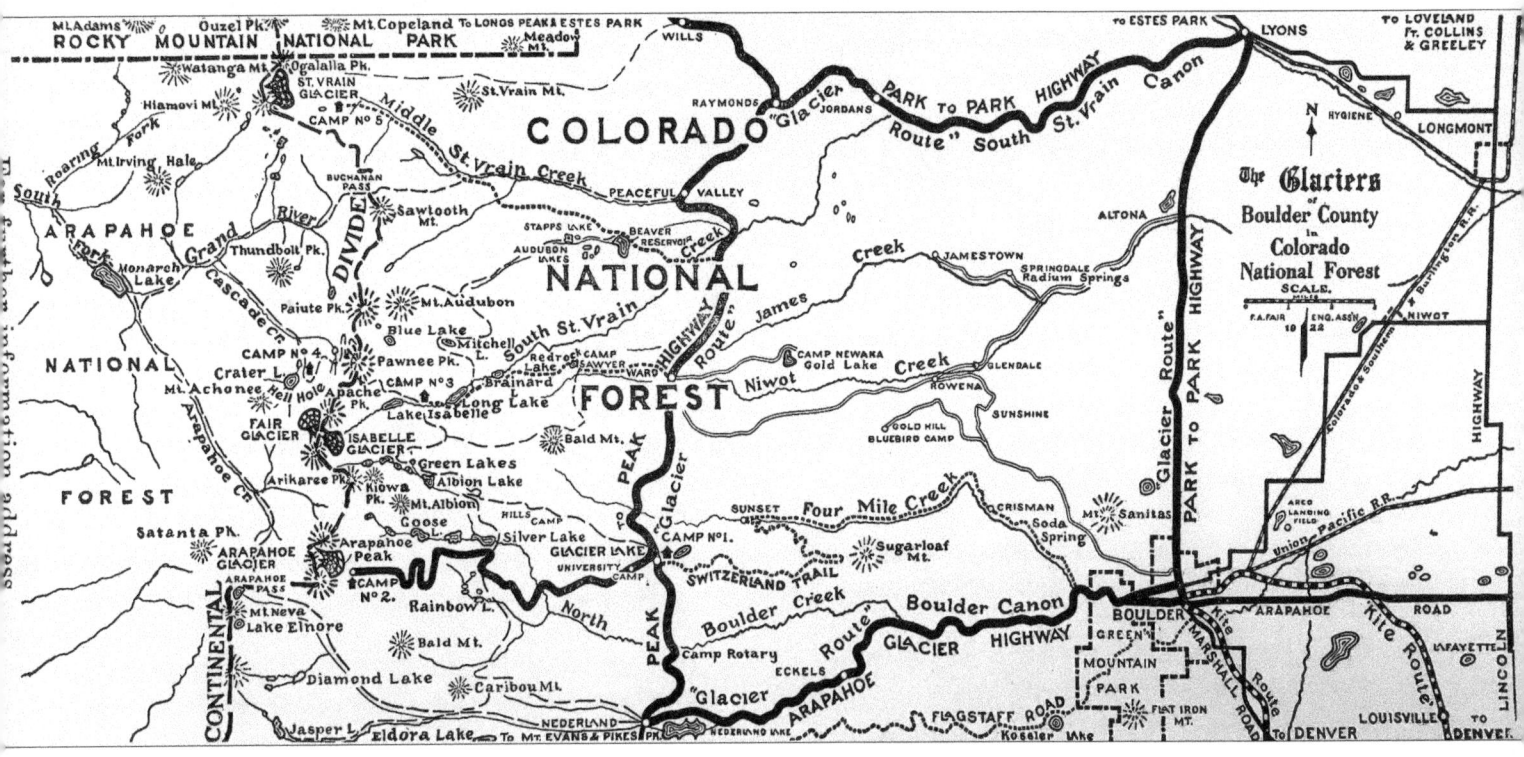

The Boulder Chamber of Commerce produced a brochure to promote the new Rainbow Lakes Road. It included this 1922 map of The Glaciers of Boulder County which shows the driving route to Arapaho Glacier. Today the Rainbow Lakes Road is also called the University of Colorado Mountain Research Station road. Note that Boulder Canyon (Boulder Cañon) between Boulder and Nederland is also labeled "Arapahoe Glacier Highway."

the Boulder County Commissioners approved a proposal by Fred Fair to build the road to the saddle south of South Arapaho Peak, where there was a striking view of the glacier and where Fair wanted to add a refreshment stand and a shelter house. Grand County agreed to build a road up the western side of Arapaho Pass to meet Boulder County's road at the top of the pass. Colorado Springs millionaire A.E. Carlton was willing to invest in the estimated $100,000 venture and proposed an 11-mile toll road.

Boulder County's road was built as far as Rainbow Lakes, northwest of Nederland, in 1924. Lack of funds canceled the rest of the project. All the money had been spent on the east side of the Divide.

Rocky Mountain Climbers Club members posed for a photograph at the top of South Arapaho Peak in 1921.

Even without his road, promoter Fred Fair found ways to bring more tourists to the glacier. The trail originally used by miners working west of Eldora had been relocated in 1922 to make it a shorter hike to the glacier than the one that starts at Rainbow Lakes, and Fair began promoting hikes to the glacier. He convinced the Denver and Interurban Company, which operated an electric line between Denver and Boulder, to adopt the name "Glacier Route," and he used seven-passenger automobiles to bring sightseers from the train to a base camp at Rainbow Lakes. After coffee and sandwiches they traveled by horseback to the glacier. They played on the ice for an hour, sliding around and throwing snowballs, and then returned to Rainbow Lakes for a cookout before the drive back to Boulder.

Not everyone was happy about the efforts to increase tourism to the glacier. The U.S. Forest Service and Rocky Mountain National Park tried to bring the Arapaho Glacier region within the park boundaries in 1925, as was originally proposed by Enos Mills. The Rocky Mountain Climbers Club and the Colorado Mountain Club also wanted to see the newly formed Rocky

Mountain National Park expanded southward to include Arapaho Glacier, which would have effectively blocked the road plans.

But many Boulder residents didn't want their glacier in Rocky Mountain National Park. They were drinking glacier water and didn't want "the czaristic National Park Service" to take over their watershed. The city of Boulder was known as the "Gateway to the Glaciers," and the chamber of commerce claimed it was the only city in the U.S. that drank glacial water. In 1929 the city council ended the controversy by buying the glacier from the federal government at $1.25 an acre for 3,900 acres.

Proud of the city-owned glacier and wanting to show it off, the Boulder Chamber of Commerce began sponsoring guided hikes to the glacier. The first year, 1938, 48 people made the hike. The next year 200 people made the trek. They carpooled through Eldora and along the North Fork of Boulder Creek to the Fourth of July campground where they were served breakfast. After a hike up to the glacier overlook, they were treated to a rock climbing exhibition by Rocky Mountain Rescue group and some descended to the glacier to play on the ice. By 1974 the popular hike attracted 600 participants.

The annual hikes on the second Sunday in August were discontinued in 1976 due in part to their massive size and the heavy environmental damage they created. Boulder Daily Camera editor Laurence Paddock noted that 14,000 people, from carried infants to 80-year-olds, had made the trek.

Over the years, Rocky Mountain National Park superintendents pushed to annex the glacier and the Indian Peaks, but it wasn't until 1978 that the bill creating the Indian Peaks Wilderness was passed by Congress and signed into law by President Jimmy Carter. The citizens of Boulder still drink water from Arapahoe Glacier, and the city's watershed below it has been fenced. People are no longer allowed on the glacier, today technically considered a snowfield, but the hike to the glacier overlook and to the top of Arapaho Pass is still renowned for its stunning wildflowers and spectacular views, which are now protected from the development so actively sought in the early part of the 20th century.

The RMCC guidelines for doing the Five Day Arapaho Tramp in 1913 required "warm underclothing, mountain shoes, rain coat or equivalent, bedding wrapped in canvas and carefully tied…Persons must be able to walk ten miles per day, must furnish references as to character and agree absolutely to obey the instructions of the guides." Five years later, the climbing gear requirements were updated to include "shoes with heavy soles, hob-nailed either high tops or low shoes with leggings; two pairs of hose, one of which is woolen; a heavy sweater or coat. Women should have a short skirt and bloomers. A great deal of energy is needlessly expended in the effort to tramp and climb in long skirts; a skirt nine to twelve inches from the ground is a comfortable walking length."

Fourth of July Mine

The boiler and horse whim still stand where the Fourth of July Mine once operated. A horse was yoked to the whim and walked in a circle to raise ore, timber, or water from the mine.

Near the junction of Arapaho Pass Trail and Arapaho Glacier Trail a rusted boiler and a few other mining artifacts remain from the Fourth of July Mine. Its colorful history began on July 4, 1872, during the Caribou silver rush, when prospector C.C. Alvord staked a claim. This claim and two others staked by Alvord were the beginning of the short boom in Eldora that really didn't start until 1892.

In September of that year the Rocky Mountain News described the Fourth of July Mine: *"It appears to be outcropping of an enormous silver ledge, literally bursting from the mountain. By actual measurement it is sixty feet in width carrying ore the entire distance that shows an assay varying from $75 to $1,000 silver per ton…The mine will afford room and material—judging from the surface indications—for a hundred thousand men to mine for generations to come…"*

The shafthouse for the Fourth of July had to be sturdy, and it was built of "huge logs, solidly anchored to withstand the terrific blizzards prevalent at that altitutde. Inside the shafthouse was a horse whim which powered the hoist and a blacksmith shop," wrote Donald C. Kemp in his book *Silver, Gold and Black Iron*. He reported that another log structure served as a boarding house and sleeping quarters for the crew, and a lean-to adjoining the north side of the bunkhouse served as a stable for the whim horse.

THEN AND NOW—Rocky Mountain Climbers Club members pitched their tents on the abandoned site of the U.S. Gold Corporation's operation during one of their hikes to Arapaho Glacier in the early 1920s. Today's trail bypasses this historic site.

A Rocky Mountain Climbers Club skier noted on the back of this photo: *"A six foot snow drift covers the platform where eighty hungry hikers received their rations last July…*
U.S. Gold Corporation, Jan. 30, 1921."

The ore was mined through a tunnel whose portal was about 500 feet directly below the shafthouse.

The U.S. Gold Corporation was organized to develop the Fourth of July Mine. It dreamed of driving a tunnel through the Continental Divide, but the expected deposits of high-grade copper and gold didn't appear.

Historian John R. Langley claimed that the mine was salted to impress prospective stockholders. *"Old Bob Stewart, the hermit prospector that lived in a tiny cabin at the head of Strawberry Creek, told me how this mine was salted. Since he lived alone miles from anyone else, he was seldom seen, except when he came to town for flour, beans and chewing tobacco; also to get drunk. Bob would go to Caribou Mine and pick out ore from the dump and pack it to the shafthouse. Some trips were made to the Boernite Mine northwest of Caribou. Each trip was a day's work. After a time there was quite a nice pile of good ore supposedly from this shaft. Prospective stock holders were shown the ore, but the mine was full of water, so they couldn't see where it came from. This hogwash must have worked pretty well, as the Fourth worked several years on the strength of it."*

THE SHAFTHOUSE—Rocky Mountain Climber Club members pose on the abandoned shafthouse at the Fourth of July Mine in 1920. South Arapaho Peak looms in the background.

ABOVE THE SHAFTHOUSE—Members of Rocky Mountain Climbers Club stop for a photo on the trail above the shafthouse of Fourth of July Mine. The shafthouse and its tall chimney sit on top of a tailings pile (center right). The building to its left is probably the boarding house.

Ancient steaming pits

Prehistoric fire pits excavated in the early 1990s from the middle of the Arapaho Pass trail contained simple flake tools and grinding slabs, leading archaeologist Jim Benedict to conclude that ancient people migrated across the Continental Divide or from lower to higher elevations each year, using the resources from many different ecosystems in the mountains.

He found one of the largest Paleo-Indian hunting camps in the Front Range in the basin where the Fourth of July Mine was located. Benedict suspected that as many as 300 fire pits may exist at the 11,000-foot-high ridge-top site at the top of the long, glacially carved valley. Many of the heavily used pits were dated 800 to 1,000 years ago. Two were carbon dated at 1,875 and 3,020 years old.

The flakes and discarded tools found at the site showed that the people who camped there used tool stones that could only have come from Western Slope quarries. Discarded sandstone grinding tools came from the hogback areas to the east, supporting the theory that Arapaho Pass was an important prehistoric travel route across the Continental Divide.

THEN AND NOW—Rocky Mountain Climbers Club hikers took a break on their trip up Arapaho Pass in 1920. This spot is easy to recognize today (opposite page).

Today's route up Arapaho Pass is shown on the map on the right. Below is a map of the "Glacier Route" Automobile Lines in Colorado from the early 1920s.

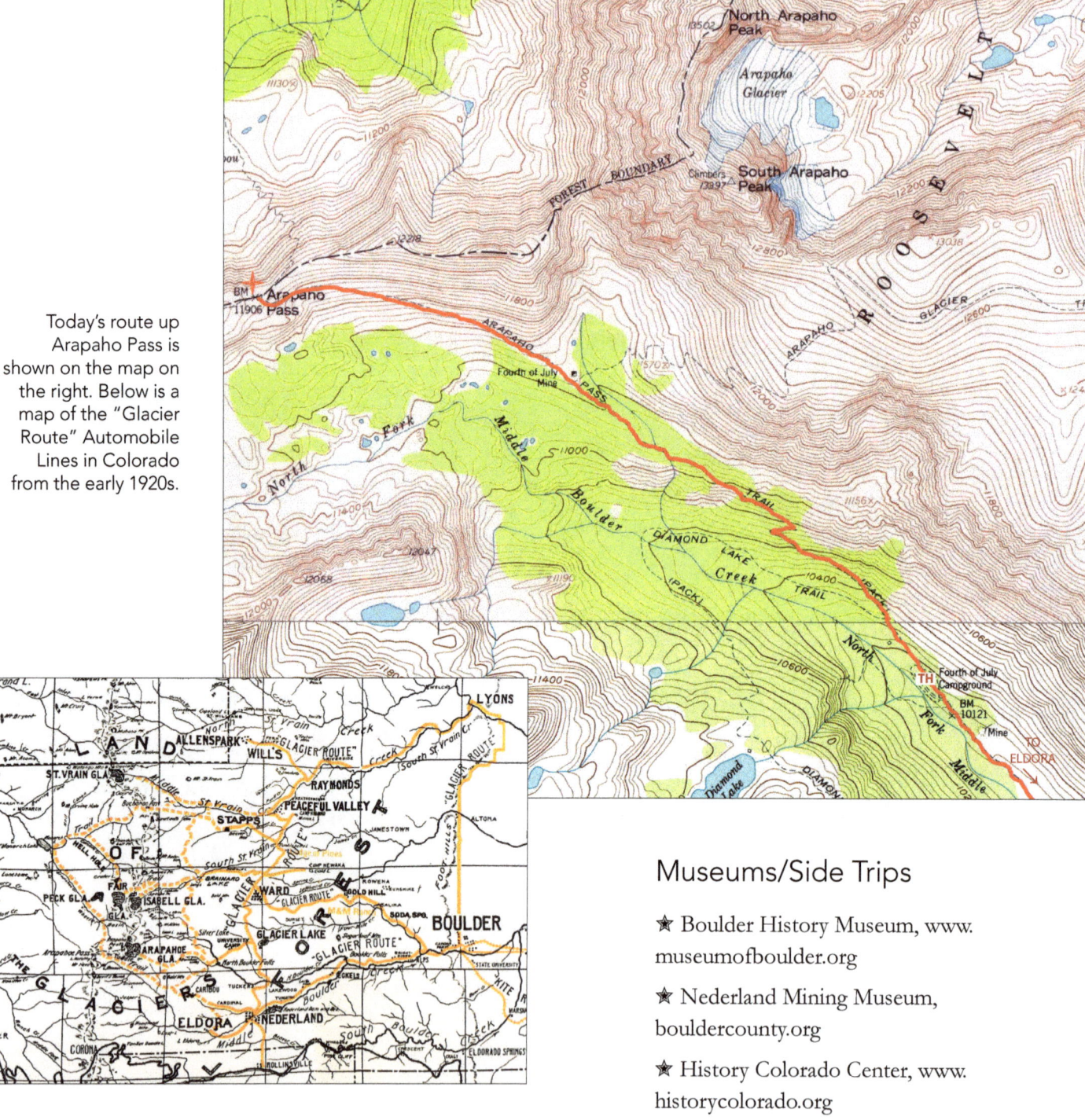

Museums/Side Trips

★ Boulder History Museum, www.museumofboulder.org

★ Nederland Mining Museum, bouldercounty.org

★ History Colorado Center, www.historycolorado.org

Above timberline on the trail to the top of Arapaho Pass.

The trail today

From the Nederland roundabout, head south on Colorado Highway 119 for 0.6 miles. Turn west onto County Road 130, signed for Eldora. Follow the paved road through the valley to the town of Eldora, where the pavement ends. Continue beyond the end of the pavement, and when the road forks, go uphill to the right. The road can be rugged past the fork. The small parking lot for the Fourth of July Trailhead fills up early, even on weekdays. The trail up Arapaho Pass starts here and climbs to the top of the pass at 11,906 feet. The trail reaches the Fourth of July Mine and the Arapaho Glacier Trail intersection at 2.1 miles. The top of the pass is another 1.2 miles. Abundant wildflowers, views of rugged peaks, and cascading waterfalls make this trail one of the most popular in Colorado. You can often hear pikas squeaking and marmots whistling at each other. Mining artifacts mark the turnoff for the glacier overlook trail. Watch for prehistoric hunting blinds and the remains of later mining activities. Beware of the possibility of afternoon thunderstorms and lightning, especially above treeline. This is a strenuous trail because of the elevation gain.

CORONA
and Rollins Pass

Corona Trip

THEN AND NOW— In 1920, Rocky Mountain Climbers Club hikers could still explore the snowsheds on top of Rollins Pass. Today's hikers see only remnants of the structures.

Top of the World

The tiny town of Corona sprang into existence in October of 1904. It perched at the very top of the Hill Route, at the end of the line that was being built over Rollins Pass to link the Front Range to the western part of the state. The line was supposed to be a temporary link until a tunnel could be built, but that would take 24 years.

The little railroad town perched above treeline at 11,660 feet at the highest point reached by a

The original depot and lunch room were enclosed by the snowshed at Corona which towered over the one-story log station building. This dimly lit tunnel was Corona's main street. All the trains had to stop at Corona to have their brakes checked, to receive orders, to switch out workers, and to let off and pick up passengers. Trains had to creep through the shed to avoid running into each other in the dark and smoke. Vents were added to the snowshed to help with the coal smoke and toxic gases that built up when several big locomotives and rotaries were in the shed at one time, which made working conditions miserable and dangerous. Workers suffered temporary blindness, loss of consciousness and sometimes death. Doorways led from the tunnel to the men's sleeping quarters, the foreman's office, and the powerhouse.

Passengers returned to a waiting eastbound train after eating at the restaurant in the Corona Hotel. A handwritten note on the bottom of the photo says, "Where we ate bear meat." Doors in the north wall of the snowshed opened to this gravel path that led to the restaurant.

Below: A panorama taken in 1909 of the view from Corona shows the long line of snowsheds, a man standing on a rock lookout, and Needle's Eye Tunnel and Jenny Lake on the right.

standard-gauge railroad in the United States. Built by David Moffat's Denver, Northeastern & Pacific Railway, the line was known as the Moffat Road.

During the years the railroad chugged its way over Rollins Pass, the crews that lived at Corona were responsible for clearing rockslides and tunnel walls that gave way. They fought fires on the high wooden trestles and repaired the snowsheds that kept avalanches off the tracks. They walked track in 30-below weather. They manned the giant rotary snowplows when blizzards howled around the peaks of the Divide and buried the tracks in 30-foot drifts. Only the hardiest of men survived. And only passengers who had to travel the route for business, mostly ranchers and lumbermen, dared to take the harrowing trip over the Hill in winter. Avalanches knocked cars off the lines or blocked the tracks, sometimes for days. Travelers could be stranded in the Corona snowshed for days, and one time almost a month.

Steel cables attached to the roof helped keep the hotel/restaurant in place when the wind blew over 100 miles an hour. The restaurant in the hotel operated for three years from 1914 to 1916. The smaller building on the right was the employees' cottage.

The number of men stationed at Corona in winter—50 to 60—shrank in the summer. Summer was easier on the crews, and warmer weather brought scores of tourists to the little town. The railroad built a pavilion where sightseers could take in the views and a hotel where they could get a room and a meal. Inside the mile-long snowshed at Corona were a café, a telegraph office, and several other businesses that catered to the tourists. Outside the snowshed, dinner could be had at Lininger's Corona Café for 50 cents.

"The Greatest One-Day Scenic Trip in the World"

The railroad's revenue from hauling coal, cattle, lumber, supplies, and equipment was heavily supplemented by the income from passenger tickets, and the railroad advertised extensively to fill its seats. Tens of thousands of colorful brochures were distributed, and the Moffat Road even used a brand new advertising medium, a motion picture, which was shown throughout the Midwest. According to an article in the Denver Republican newspaper in

An early day billboard at the Jenny Lake siding exhorted passengers to "Telegraph Your Friends from Corona, Highest Standard Gauge Station in the World." A train descends from Corona in the background. This photo was taken by newlyweds Idelia and Milton Baumgarten on their honeymoon in 1924.

August 1905, "The amusement enterprise company which will use this series of Moffat Road pictures has show houses built in imitation of a [railroad] passenger car. People enter this car as in a theater and…the effects are such that it appears that the car starts to move. There is a curtain in the front end of the car and it appears the car is being pushed by an engine and scenery displayed on the curtain flits before the eyes as if viewed from an ordinary observation car."

The result of all this advertising was an unbelievable amount of tourist travel. Not only did tourists come from out of state, but many Denver-area residents also wanted to take the inexpensive trip to the Top of the World. "The mind-boggling scenic attractions were countless. The solitary world of the alpine tundra, where there was nothing between man and the sky and where the wind blew one's voice away, just awed the traveler…" The railroad built restaurants at Tolland, Corona, and Arrow, the next town built as the tracks continued past Corona and down the western side of Rollins Pass. It stocked the streams along the Moffat Road with fish. A dancing pavilion was added at Tolland so tourists would have a diversion between arrivals and departures of the trains. The railroad town of Tolland was at the base of what was called the Giant's Ladder, like the one on the route to Mont Alto, where the railroad zig-zagged up the mountainside along a route that looked like enormous rungs. A commuter train traveled between Denver and Tolland every day for those who had summer cabins in South Boulder Canyon. Excursion trains often operated in two or three sections on summer Sundays.

Thriving excursion business was stimulated by a new ticket office in downtown Denver, and excursions were offered for conventions, church groups, employee groups, and wildflower gathering. The biggest excursion was the grocer's special that brought 3,000 passengers in 11 sections for a day in the mountains. It was a dispatching triumph with 11 trains of borrowed locomotives, crews, and coaches that were loaded in Denver and turned around on the Y-shaped section of track at Arrow.

A commercial photographer at Corona usually posed groups of women or family groups with handfuls of snow and a sign that read, "Top of the World, Corona." When the tourist trains stopped at Tolland a list of passenger names was given to a printer, and as the train continued to Corona or Arrow the Moffat Road Daily Reporter was printed, listing the names of all the passengers who went to the Top of the World that day. When the train returned through Tolland, the newspaper was distributed to the tourists.

When the tunnel under the Divide was finally completed in February of 1928 Corona was abandoned. Any material or equipment that was worth salvaging was loaded onto freight trains, and the railroad men packed their belongings and boarded a Denver-bound train.

The tracks over Rollins Pass were not immediately dismantled and remained usable as an emergency route, a good thing when several wooden planks inside the Moffat Tunnel collapsed in July 1928. Sometime in the seven years between when the line was abandoned and when the tracks were removed in 1935, a mysterious fire destroyed several snowsheds near the summit as well as the hotel at Corona Station.

The remnants of Corona remind us of a time when hardy railroad workers toiled tirelessly above treeline to keep the Hill Route open and tourists flocked by the tens of thousands to ogle the spectacular scenery and have their photos taken at the Top of the World.

Telegraph poles were shortened to withstand the winds at Corona, and railroad men sometimes followed the poles that stuck out of the snow to find their way when snow drifted over the 22-foot-high snowshed. The twin stacks for the boilers and power plant were built during the winter of 1915-16.

Railroad workers who manned one of the rotary plows on the Moffat Road stopped briefly for a photo.

THEN AND NOW
On a trip in 1920, members of the Rocky Mountain Climbers Club rested at the gazebo that was built by the U.S. Forest Service next to the railroad tracks and overlooked the east side of the pass. Below: The structure is no more than a pile of logs today, but the view that drew tens of thousands of tourists is still spectacular.

THEN AND NOW
Opposite page, top: Vents poked up from the top of the 3,650-foot-long Corona snowshed in this 1914 photo. The roof of the gazebo can be seen on the far right. A foot bridge crossed over the top of the snowshed, and a gravel path led to the hotel/restaurant. The smaller building was the employee's cottage, and between them was the hotel's water tank. Below is the same scene today.

Perpetual snow at Corona was one of its major attractions. Excursionists threw snowballs, rode burros, and posed for photos, including the author's great-aunt and great-uncle, the couple on the left.

A daring descent

Top: Marjorie Perry and her friend Elinor Eppich Kingery (below) got off the train at Corona and skied down the tracks to Ladora. Marjorie's father was involved with the construction of the Moffat Tunnel (note the railroad patch on her coat), and Elinor became a well-respected mountaineer, historian, and author. Marjorie was instrumental in promoting the ski industry in Colorado, and Greenwood Village is named after her farm on Greenwood Ranch.

Just days before the Moffat Tunnel opened and rail travel over the Hill Route ceased forever, Marjorie Perry and her friend Elinor Eppich [later Kingery] got off the train when it stopped at Corona and skied down the tracks to Ladora.

Perry and Eppich were experienced mountaineers and skiers. Marjorie frequently rode the Moffat Road between her cabin in the Steamboat Springs area and her farm home in Denver.

When Marjorie heard the conductor say the train would be stopped at Corona for a couple of hours, she roused her companion, and the two gathered their ski equipment. They were coming back from a week spent skiing with a Norwegian friend, Lars Haugen (see page 20) after the Steamboat Springs Winter Carnival. The weather on that particular day in February 1928 was unusually temperate—the sun was shining and the wind not howling quite as much as usual. Marjorie thought the two women could descend 2,000 feet on the east side of the Continental Divide into the valley of South Boulder Creek and have the train pick them up.

Marjorie said the tracks were cleared *"but between them was a packed trail and we slid easily into motion as we hit it. Around the grade we spun—not too fast—just moving along friskily. The hillside was very steep as we wound around the mountain, hardly daring to look at the bottom of the draw…I knew about the trestle where a deep crevasse cut into the sidehill, but I had always seen it from the cozy coach where getting over it was not my responsibility. We were suddenly scared, but now*

Climbing up one of the icy supports inside a snowshed would have been tricky, but Marjorie and Elinor figured they could do it if they had to. The lights at the top of the shed were from the vents. The women skied through six snowsheds and fortunately didn't meet a train inside any of them.

the rugged hillside was impossible to scale. Elinor had those horrible ski bindings that wrapped around and around, so she left her skis on. I took mine off [Marjorie's skis were eight feet long], crawled on my hands and knees and she hung onto me. Without the fierce wind it wouldn't have been so bad, but it was a long way down! Thanks goodness, it was only about 200 feet long and then we went gaily on."

The women skied through several short snowsheds, and then approached one that was perhaps a half mile long. Marjorie was becoming increasingly frantic because she knew that the snow plow was coming up the tracks toward them, clearing the tracks for the train to descend from Corona. If they were inside the snowshed when they met it, they could get caught in the meat grinder of a rotary plow.

They decided that if that happened they would climb an icy support to get up under the roof. Marjorie figured Elinor could push her up and then Marjorie could pull Elinor up with her skis on. *"At last we came out into the open, the hillside was not so steep, and we could see where the track made a switchback. Right there, we left the beaten track just as the rotary plow chugged up the hill past us. With horror, Elinor watched those grinding metals turn and throw the snow high over the bank. It would make pulp of anything in its path."*

In this photograph a Denver & Salt Lake train approached Tolland from the east (right side of photo), and three trains worked their way along the Giant's Ladder, the route skied by Marjorie and Elinor. People milled about between the dance pavilion (the building the engine is just passing) and the depot, concession stand, ice house, lunch counter, and other businesses. A rock wall protected the businesses from the noise and smoke of the railroad. This photo was taken in the early 1900s.

The women got back in the track, lifted their poles, and were blown by the wind to Jenny Lake in no time, where they met the train again. Since the track ahead was clear they decided to continue their ski *"so we just set sail and went. As we sped along past the section house, the little man with a broom opened his mouth but no sound came forth, he was so astonished. Occasionally we had to brake with our poles for the wind seemed stronger and we felt as if were flying as the big pine trees sped by."* Past the flag station of Antelope they could see tiny Tolland far below. They left the track and went *"straight down the hill making big curves with the perfect powder snow swirling in the air."*

Instead of going to Tolland, which they could see was icy and blown bare, the women skied on to Ladora. They waited about a half hour for the train, and were welcomed aboard by several women from Boston who had volunteered to watch their belongings. Twenty years after their adventure, Marjorie wrote that *"It had taken place when skiers were a curiosity and skiing as a sport was in its infancy in Colorado."* And since the tunnel opened several days after their adventure, the thrill of the trip was theirs alone. ✻

The trestle near Ladora where Marjorie and Elinor waited for the train to pick them up.

The edge of this trestle near Corona floats high above the valleys below. When Marjorie and Elinor skied over this trestle high winds threatened to send them over the edge, so Marjorie crawled over the trestle, and Elinor held onto her so she didn't have to take her skis off.

After a fire in October of 1918 the railroad brought in boxcar bodies for bunk houses, the telegraph office, and other buildings at Corona. A 106-foot-long covered wooden passageway connected them to the snowshed on one end and to a frame lunch room and dining room at the other end.

Smoke and fumes made it dangerous to go for a walk inside the snowshed at Corona, so people often took walks along the top of the shed.

The White Desert was filmed on location at Rollins Pass and the Continental Divide at Corona. Released in 1925, it was a propaganda film to win public support for the building of the Moffat Tunnel, which would eliminate the treacherous and unreliable rail service over the pass. A 35mm copy of *The White Desert* is preserved at the George Eastman House, and it is still shown occasionally in Colorado. Other movies filmed on Moffat Road include *Switchback,* some of which was shot near Rollinsville, Tolland, and Pinecliffe, and background for *Under Seige 2: Dark Territory,* which was filmed near Pinecliffe.

Museums/Side Trips

★ Colorado Railroad Museum, Golden Colorado; coloradorailroadmuseum.org

★ Cozens Ranch Museum and Stage Stop, Fraser, Colorado; grandcountyhistory.org

★ Pioneer Village Museum, Hot Sulphur Springs, Colorado; grandcountyhistory.org

★ Moffat Road Railroad Museum, Granby, Colorado; the building for this new museum was still in progress in early 2019, but the Interpretive Park was already open; moffatroadrailroadmuseum.org

From the lower snowshed at Yankee Doodle Lake the railroad track gained about 600 feet to the snowshed at the top of the photo, which was at the west side of the Needle's Eye Tunnel.

Top: This is the same snowshed from the opposite page in summer. Below: A train leaves the Needle's Eye Tunnel as it heads east toward the Giant's Ladder and Tolland.

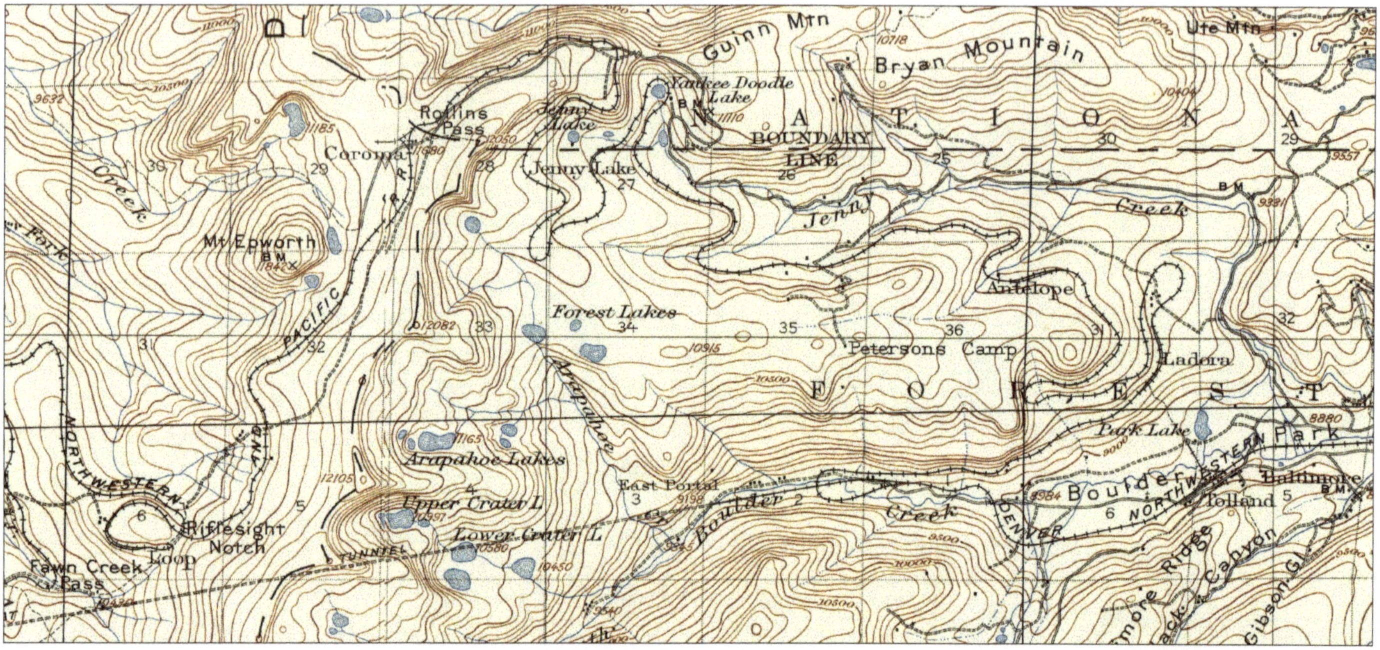
Guinn Mtn
Bryan Mountain
Ute Mtn
Yankee Doodle Lake
Rollins Pass
Jenny Lake
Corona
BOUNDARY LINE
Jenny Lake
Jenny Creek
Mt Epworth
PACIFIC
Forest Lakes
Antelope
Petersons Camp
Ladora
Arapahoe
Park Lake
Arapahoe Lakes
NORTHWESTERN
Upper Crater L
Lower Crater L
East Portal
Boulder Creek
Riflesight Notch
Loop
Fawn Creek Pass
TUNNEL
Park
Baltimore
Tolland
DENVER
NORTHWESTERN
Ridge
Canyon
Gibson Gl

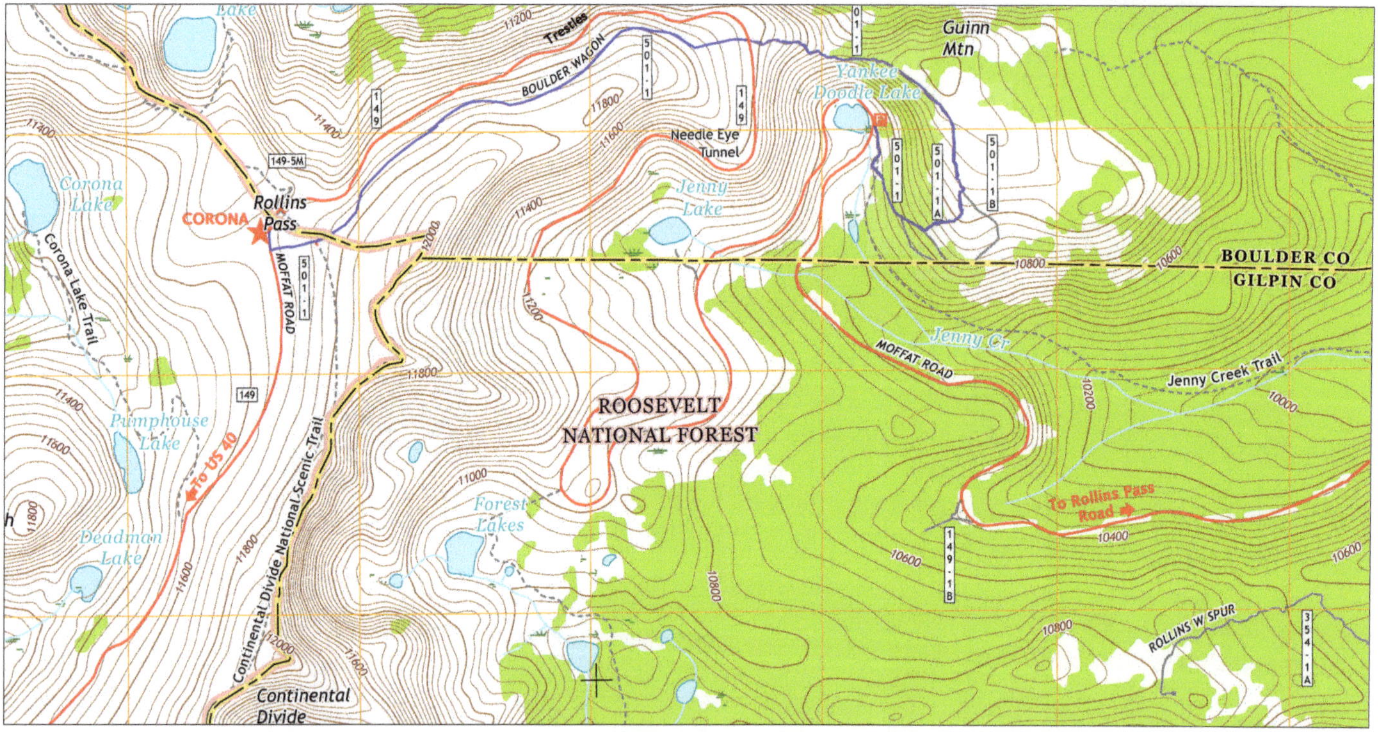
Guinn Mtn
Trestles
BOULDER WAGON
Yankee Doodle Lake
Needle Eye Tunnel
Jenny Lake
Corona Lake
CORONA
Rollins Pass
MOFFAT ROAD
Corona Lake Trail
BOULDER CO
GILPIN CO
Jenny Cr
MOFFAT ROAD
Jenny Creek Trail
ROOSEVELT NATIONAL FOREST
Pumphouse Lake
To US 40
Deadman Lake
Continental Divide National Scenic Trail
Forest Lakes
To Rollins Pass Road
ROLLINS W SPUR
Continental Divide

THEN AND NOW
The 1912 map on the opposite page shows the route of the railroad and the summit of Rollins Pass where the railroad built the town of Corona. The route of today's road doesn't deviate much from that route. Right: All that remains of Corona are foundations and memories of dreams.

The trail today

To get to Corona from the west side of the pass, drive south from Winter Park on U.S. Highway 40 approximately one mile to County Road 80 (Forest Road 149) and turn left. Drive 15 miles on the dirt road to the site of Corona. There is a small parking area near the collapsed viewing pavilion. This road is generally open from mid-June to mid-November.

From the east side of the pass, turn off Colorado Highway 119 (Peak to Peak Scenic Byway) in Rollinsville (five miles south of Nederland) and head west up Rollins Pass Road. For a small side trip, you can drive past the turnoff for the Moffat Road and check out the East Portal of the Moffat Tunnel, which made the railroad over the Hill obsolete. The turnoff for the Moffat Road is just before East Portal. From here the narrow dirt road is rarely maintained, and it can be quite rugged. The road is a narrow corridor between Indian Peaks Wilderness and James Peak Wilderness, neither of which allows motorized vehicles or bikes, and vehicles must stay on the road or face a $5,000 fine. Drive 15 miles to Needle's Eye Tunnel, which is closed, and find a wide spot to park. There is a very steep detour trail over the tunnel. Continue on the old rail bed, and you will cross two of the original trestles, which remain in fair condition. For an alternate route, you can park at Yankee Doodle Lake and hike the Boulder Wagon Trail from the east side of the lake to Corona (route shown in blue on the map.) This route is closed to vehicular traffic and also has some very steep sections. Make this into a loop hike by traveling Moffat Road one direction and Boulder Wagon Road in the other, returning to your car at Yankee Doodle Lake. It's a two to four-mile hike from the tunnel to Corona depending on the route you take. Either route is a strenuous hike for advanced hikers in great shape.

Dress warmly to explore Corona and remember the elevation is 11,660 feet. It's a windswept, barren landscape above treeline, and afternoon thunderstorms often bring lightning with them. Foundations from the town and the hotel remain, as does fallen timber from collapsed snowsheds. It's not difficult to imagine just how thrilling the train ride was over Rollins Pass when you're hiking the abandoned rail bed and exploring the old townsite.

THEN AND NOW Pumphouse Lake was a favorite spot for Rocky Mountain Climbers Club members, shown here on a hike in 1920. Below: The lake looks the same today.

Winter Park Ski Area is visible from the trailhead for the short hike to Pumphouse Lake.

Bonus hike

In July and August you can take a quick hike down to Pumphouse Lake. The trail starts just west of the Corona townsite on the Rollins Pass Road at the sign for the Corona Lake Trail. It's about a half mile down to the small lake that provided water for the Corona Station, the hotel, and the railroad water tanks. Water was pumped up to Corona by a steam-generated water pump. The water pump operator and his wife spent the winter here, isolated except for the telegraph.

Caribou

Wind and Wealth

THEN AND NOW— The views above the townsite of Caribou are as spectacular today as they were when these women posed for a photograph in the late 1800s.

Tales of fabulous wealth

The sloping high mountain meadow nestled below the remains of once-famous mines was at one time a bustling community, with busy streets, children running home from school, stages coming and going with mail and passengers, and the constant cacophony of mills extracting gold and silver from the huge mines.

In its 35 years of existence Caribou was famous throughout the country for its vast reserves of silver which were discovered by a hunting party

Idaho Street businesses included Werley's Saloon, far left, which offered men in the camp a chance to relax with friends, play billiards, or gamble. Next to it was the post office, buttressed against the wind by long poles, then Scott Bros. and Herzinger & Harter, which sold general merchandise and some groceries. The once proud buildings showed the effects of the harsh high-altitude sun, brutal winters, and winds of Caribou.

in 1860. Reports of "the greatest silver vein in the region" brought droves of prospectors to the area, and Caribou City was established in 1870. It soon grew to a thriving community of 60 businesses and 400 people, supported by 20 producing mines. At its peak, Caribou was home to 1,000 people.

Stories of fabulous wealth spread. The miners who staked the Idaho claim reportedly took out more than $6,000 from a 20-foot shaft in one month. It was reported that specimens from the Caribou vein assayed as high as 10,000 ounces of silver to the ton. The Caribou Mine produced an estimated $8 million worth of silver, which made it one of Colorado's greatest producers.

President Ulysses S. Grant walked on silver bricks from the Caribou Mine in 1873 when he visited Central City. Exhibits of Caribou silver at the 1876 Philadelphia Centennial Exposition attracted the attention of the world, and more men crowded into town. Mail ar-

Women were greatly outnumbered by men in Caribou. For this photograph a few of them stopped on the boardwalk on Idaho Street, probably in front of the church, which was located next to a brewery and the telegraph office. Murphy's meat market and dance hall (with the upper balcony) and two more saloons farther down the street catered to the entertainment needs of the camp's men, as did Werley's Saloon, the first building on the left side of the street.

rived daily from Boulder, and three times a week from Central City. One of the first businesses to open was the Caribou Post newspaper, which published once a week from May 27, 1871, to Aug. 17, 1872.

But at 10,000 feet above sea level, life in Caribou was not easy. Epidemics of scarlet fever and diphtheria swept through town and took the lives of many children. In the winter snowstorms buried buildings, sometimes for weeks at a time. In the spring and summer thunderstorms rolled across the skies alarmingly close to town, and violent winds blasted through town at any time of year, making it hard to breathe and threatening to demolish everything in sight.

Caribou was known as "the town where the winds were born," and when the wind blew in Nederland, four miles to the east, it was said that "someone in Caribou must have left the door open." When a newcomer asked when summer would arrive, a miner in Werley's Saloon was heard to say, "Don't know, I've only been here three years." Old timers told of winters so brutal that a thick rope was fastened at one end near the center of town and at the other to the Caribou Shafthouse. A man was safe as long as he could hold the rope, but some who let go lost their way and were "never seen again."

Fire leveled most of the mine buildings in 1879. Fires had been burning on Arapaho Peak for a couple of weeks, and on Sunday, Sept. 14, Caribou's citizens woke to a smoky sky. That afternoon a wind de-

THEN AND NOW
Caribou's packed dirt streets were dusty and muddy, and the town installed water and sanitation systems in the 1870s. The school house is the white building at the lower left. The large white building in the center front is the Sherman House hotel. It's at the end of the business block of Idaho Street. Three stories high, the Sherman House had 28 sleeping rooms, a parlor, a large dining room, and a reading room. The Boulder County News reported that guests were treated to "carpeted floors, black walnut furnishings, and sheets, pillows and coverlets white as the driven snow" along with "homelike meals" and "genuine good coffee." The Sherman was Caribou's social center for a number of years.

The mines of Caribou were idle in 1880 due to a slump in the silver market, but they were working again when this photo was taken closer to 1900. The shafthouse and waste dump of the great Caribou Mine are in the center of the photograph. Just under the Caribou is the Poorman, another of Caribou's famous mines. At left are the No Name and the Sherman (partially masked). The small shafthouse on the horizon to the right is the Belcher Mine.

George Lytle discovered the famous and lucrative Poorman Mine. It was later owned and developed by Sam Conger. Lytle, Conger, and William Martin are credited for the discovery of silver at Caribou.

scribed as a perfect gale swept the fire up Caribou Hill. A frantic effort on the hoists brought miners to the surface, but then the fire turned and raced over Idaho Hill and into town. Hundreds of cords of wood had been stacked next to buildings in anticipation of winter, and the fire ran from house to house, forcing women and children to flee, many leaving everything behind. The town's new water system and bucket brigades saved many of the buildings in the business district, but numerous homes were lost.

Boulder and Central City rallied to help the stricken town, but many of Caribou's citizens didn't rebuild. The mines had begun to play out, silver crashed in 1893, and Caribou began to decline. The town suffered through a few more small fires and an earthquake, and the population continued to dwindle.

In 1905 another major fire leveled the Sherman House, the church, and Murphy's meat market. The south part of town was destroyed, and Caribou never rebuilt or recovered. By 1910 only 51 people lived in Caribou, and today one miner, Tom Hendricks, continues to work the famous ore deposits.

THEN AND NOW
The New Jersey Mill was built in Caribou in 1876 and was launched with a flourish a year later. It was forced to shut down after just two weeks because of a scarcity of ore. It was one of several mills that was a victim of Eastern investors not understanding the difficulties of operating in such an isolated and hostile environment. The New Jersey was built as the mines in Caribou were playing out, and there never was enough ore to keep it solvent. The rock foundation at the far right of the building in the above photo taken in 1897 is all that remains at the site today (left).

No. 264. CARIBOU from the WEST.

The fortunes of Caribou were declining in the early 1890s. The price of silver had plummeted from $1.27 an ounce in 1874 to 63 cents in 1894. Across the U.S. the financial crisis that created the Panic of 1893 ruined thousands of businesses, and more than four million people were left unemployed. As fortunes in Caribou declined, residents helped each other out, often leaving fresh meat or other food for neighbors in need. Many residents kept a cow or a few chickens and some planted gardens, a challenge at Caribou's high altitude. The Sherman House is the large white building just to the right of center in this photo.

A mysterious disappearance

On a blustery, blizzardy Sunday morning in May of 1893, Caribou school teacher T.H. Bernard put on his overcoat and told some of the school boys that he was going for a walk.

He started over Idaho Hill and never came back.

Bernard was known as "a young man of good habits" who was "accustomed to take long walks." He had only one week remaining in his teaching contract and had $40 coming to him from the school district. The general consensus was that he had no reason not to come back.

Townspeople organized relief parties on Monday and searched in the blinding snowstorms which would have covered any tracks that Bernard may have made. They examined every prospect hole they could, but they didn't find any trace of the young man.

A few days later the weather cleared, and searchers found footprints that they followed up the flanks of Arapaho Peak. The footprints disappeared at the edge of a deep precipice. It was reported in the Boulder newspaper that *"These cravasses in the banks of eternal snow are covered up by late snows and a thin roof forms over them at places. It is the theory that Bernard stepped on this roof or in the blinding snowstorm he did not see the great cravasse and walked into it and fell to the bottom, where a rivulet runs through the banks of snow to Boulder creek. Men left Caribou yesterday with axes, shovels and ropes and prepared to let some of their number down into the ravine."*

The searchers came back empty-handed. It seemed that Bernard had truly disappeared.

When school teacher Bernard disappeared in 1893, far fewer students attended the school in Caribou than are pictured here. One tale told of a big range bull knocking down one of the poles that propped the building against the wind while using it as a back scratcher. The wind then came along, lifted the building and set it down again at a right angle to its original position.

In the meantime, W.S. Rothermel, a well-known mining expert, arrived in Boulder, where he got a room at the German House. Professor Rothermel had discovered mines by the "affinity" system and believed in his power to locate anything. He had every confidence that he could find the lost teacher, and all he required was something the man had recently worn. When the professor arrived in Caribou he was handed a pair of shoes that Bernard, the lost teacher, had left in his room. After a little deliberation, Rothermel indicated a spot on a map that was about two miles beyond Central City where he said Bernard was lying with his right leg broken and his face turned toward Caribou.

Murphy's meat market and butcher shop also housed a popular dance hall on the second floor. It and the Sherman House were the two most popular venues for the frequent dances which often lasted through the night, with a break for lunch around midnight.

"I will give you $50 if you will go there and find Bernard," said Mayor Cowie. "And I'll give you another $50," said Mr. Russell. "Well," said P.J. Werley, owner of Werley's Saloon and town clerk, "I'll make it $100 more." At this point, reported the Boulder newspaper, Henry Lippoldt offered to provide a team and driver for the trip to retrieve the body, "but the gentleman was too busy to go."

The mystery of the missing school teacher was not solved until December of 1905, when miner John Williams found a skull at the base of a 200-foot cliff on Arapaho Peak. He brought the skull to Eldora, and it was identified as Bernard's by the gold work in the teeth.

THEN AND NOW
The Potosi Mining Company refurbished one of Caribou's business buildings in the late 1920s as a rooming and boarding house. Today, it is one of two remains of stone buildings in Caribou.

Mount Thorodin and the area around Nederland are part of the view to the east from the meadow where the town of Caribou once thrived.

The Caribou Brass Band, sometimes referred to as the Silver Cornet Band, played for Caribou's Christmas and New Year's Eve balls in 1871. They were in demand for dances, parties, weddings, and serenades. The band also traveled to nearby communities, including Boulder. Caribou also supported a string band.

When President Ulysses S. Grant came to Central City in 1873, the city was eager to outdo the other mining towns on the president's itinerary. It decided to pave the entrance to the Teller House hotel, where the president and the first lady would walk from their carriage, with silver instead of gold, which was far too common in Central. The city brought $12,000 worth of silver bricks over the mountains from Caribou, and the only thing that marred the president's walk across them was the small boys who threw snowballs. The bricks weighed approximately 70 pounds each and measured about 13x4x4 inches.

This family portrait was framed with the thriving town of Caribou in the background. The woman leaning against the tree is also in photographs on pages 91 and 96.

As Caribou declined, its mines and mills still loomed over the remaining buildings.

Museums/Side Trips

★ Nederland Mining Museum, bouldercounty.org

★ Cardinal Mill tour, bouldercounty.org

The trail today

At the roundabout in Nederland take the spur toward Ward and drive almost a half-mile to the left turn for County Road 128. This is a dirt road that winds its way steadily uphill about five miles to the old townsite of Caribou. There is a parking area above the stone ruins. The trail to the old stone wall that was part of the New Jersey Mill traverses the meadow, starting below the parking area. This meadow that is today filled with wildflowers is where the old town of Caribou once prospered and at one time was home to 1,000 people. The rock wall that was part of the New Jersey mill is overgrown and just visible below the trail. If you're interested in a longer hike, continue to National Forest System Road 505 and turn right. Stay right at the next intersection, and you will return to the parking area. This is about a three-mile loop. Please stay on the trails and don't pick the wildflowers.

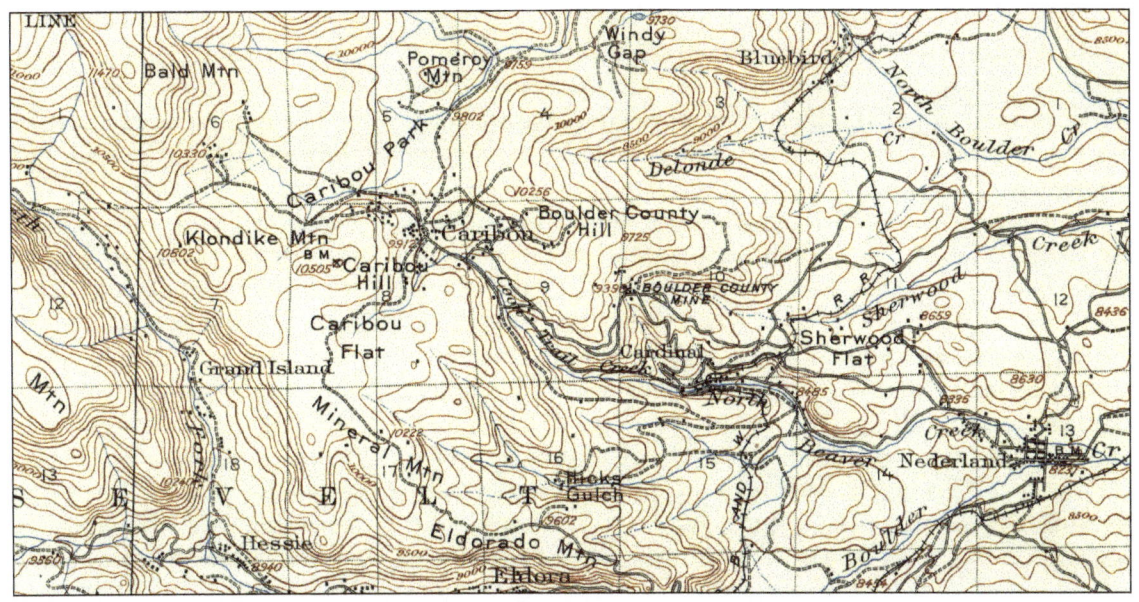

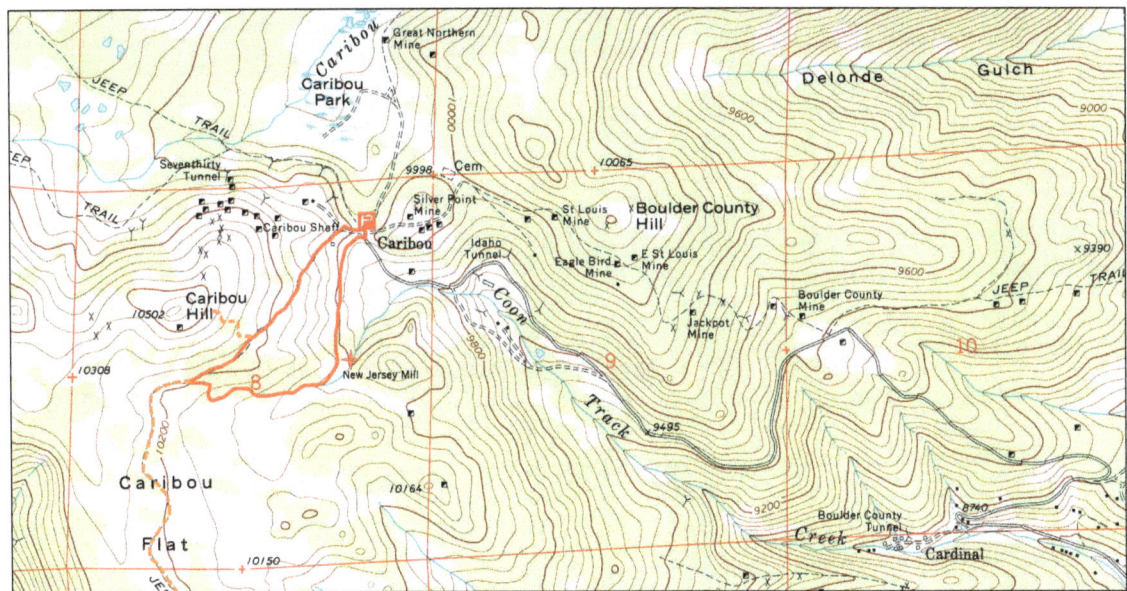

THEN AND NOW
Above: A 1912 map. Below: A modern-day map with the hike to the remains of the New Jersey Mill highlighted. Extend your hike by heading south to Caribou Flat or by hiking to the top of Caribou Hill.

LOST LAKE

THEN AND NOW—One hundred years ago Rocky Mountain Climbers Club hikers trekked to Lost Lake for the views and the fishing, the same as today.

Lost dreams at Lost Lake

Lost Lake isn't lost any more. Today's hikers go there for the stunning scenery, but in the late 1800s it was gold that brought miners to the shores of the little lake west of Eldora.

Prospectors spread out in the hills above Eldora seeking their fortunes, and mines popped up on the steep slopes above Lost Lake. The little mining camp housed as many as 200 peo-

Mines and mills used a lot of wood for power and heat, and getting the wood to the mines could be challenging. In this photo, not all of the logs that were skidded down a 30-foot snowdrift behind the Revenge Mine made it to the shafthouse. Just below the mine, sleds pulled by horses passed during winter, bringing lumber from the Woodland Flats mill to Central City. The treacherous winter route was shorter, but it was usable only when there was enough snow for the sleds. It wound along the side of Bryan Mountain, then east to the gap between Bryan and Ute mountains, through the gap west of Peterson's Lake, down Deadman's Gulch, Jenny Creek and Boulder Park, up Jenny Lind Gulch to Apex, along Pine Creek and finally into Central City. The heavy sleds were loaded with about 10,000 feet of lumber, and drawn by eight horses. Only the best drivers used the winter route.

ple in the summer months. For a few short years the Lost Lake mines, including the Norway, the Revenge, and the Shirley, were productive. But the gold boom at Lost Lake was short, as it was in Eldora. One of the bigger mining operations, the Revenge, operated from 1897 to 1907, but it only prospered for the first few of those years.

Among the sad tales about fortunes lost is the one about a mine foreman's attempt to keep the "high-grade" ore from a mine near Lost Lake for himself. He fired the men who worked in that part of the mine and leased it for himself, and he hired a man with poor eyesight to sort the ore from that area. Any remarks about a strike of rich ore were frowned on and soft-pedalled. Unfortunately for the foreman, when the mine was closed down, the supposed cache of rich ore was buried under tons of waste. The foreman moved to another camp—without his high-grade ore.

Top: The shell of one of the mine buildings at Lost Lake perches precariously on its rock foundation. Bottom: Gold ore from the Revenge was processed at the Norway Mill, which was built beside the dump at the Revenge with tracks leading from the tunnel portal directly to the mill. Left: This friction steam hoist, complete except for its control levers, was used in the mill.

Like the trail to Lost Lake, many of today's trails follow old roads. When the roads were built in the late 1800s, logs were set across the wet sections to make them passable, and they were called "corduroy roads."

Lost Lake never became more than a mining camp, and miners working at the Lost Lake mines had to go down the mountain to the towns of Hessie or Eldora for groceries and other supplies.

Eldora has survived and is now a Historic District, but almost nothing remains of Hessie, although at one time the two towns were rivals for miners' business.

Also remaining is the road the miners used to travel between the camps. Today it's traveled by those who seek scenery and history, and it has been in continuous use by hikers and skiers since mining's golden years.

Lost Lake was as popular for fishing and picnicking a hundred years ago as it is today.

THEN—F. M. Strawhum staked the Revenge Mine on Aug. 18, 1897. The mine clung to the steep mountainside above Lost Lake. About three miles west of Eldora, the Revenge never produced on its early promise. The access was difficult and the mine was often flooded, and it closed in 1907.

NOW—Lost Lake sparkles below an abandoned mine site.

Champ Smith

Mining camp murder

The mining camp of Hessie sprang up at the junction of two forks of Boulder Creek. Captain J.H. Davis founded the town and named it after his wife, who served as its postmaster. In addition to the post office, which operated for four years from 1898 to 1902, Hessie had a couple of stores, a busy sawmill, and a school. Hessie's population was reported to have grown to a high of 80 in 1901.

Twelve years after the post office closed, not many people remained in the small community. One of them was veteran miner Champ Smith, a tall, gray-haired, blue-eyed bachelor in his early 50s. On June 13, 1914, a neighbor, G.W. Orear, came to visit Smith, who was at work extending the Caledonia tunnel, about a half mile below town. Orear was also delivering Smith's mail from Eldora.

Orear found a horrific scene. Just inside the tunnel were his friend's remains. Smith had been blown apart in an explosion that left a crater inside the mine. The scene was so grisly that Orear ran the two miles back to Eldora without stopping.

Not everyone thought Smith's death was an accident. He had recently been appointed to the post of deputy game warden, and lost friends when he declared that he would uphold laws that required hunting licenses.

Top: What remained of Hessie in 1920. Bottom: Wilson Davis, one of the miners accused of murdering Champ Smith, at the Delaware Mine.

The sheriff's department's investigator collected all the bone fragments from the mud inside the tunnel and carefully washed them in the creek. He found a bullet hole in one of the pieces, about the size of the bullet he dug out of the wall. He also found blood on an ore car, and a 200-foot trail of blood leading to the site of the blast. He figured that Smith had been shot inside the tunnel, and his body was transported on the ore car closer to the portal, where, the investigator postulated, Smith's killer had set his corpse on a charge of dynamite, probably in an attempt to destroy the evidence of the murder.

Three local miners, Wilson Davis and two brothers named Smalley, were arrested for the crime, but they were set free due to a lack of evidence tying them to the case, and to this day the murder remains unsolved.

Museums/Side Trips

✹ Boulder History Museum; www.museumofboulder.org

✹ History Colorado Center; www.historycolorado.org

✹ Nederland Mining Museum; www.bouldercounty.org

Top: The Hessie Trailhead.
Bottom: Mining artifacts above the lake.

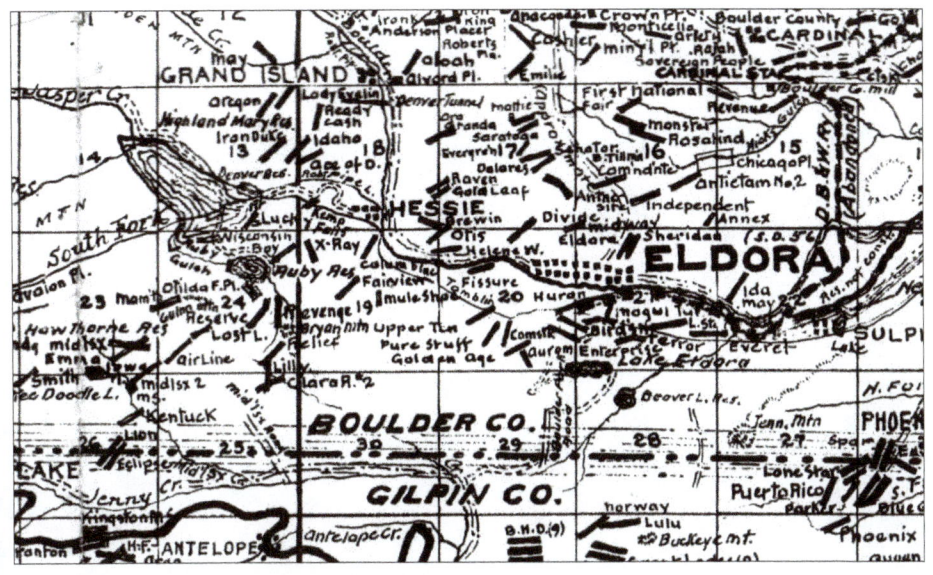

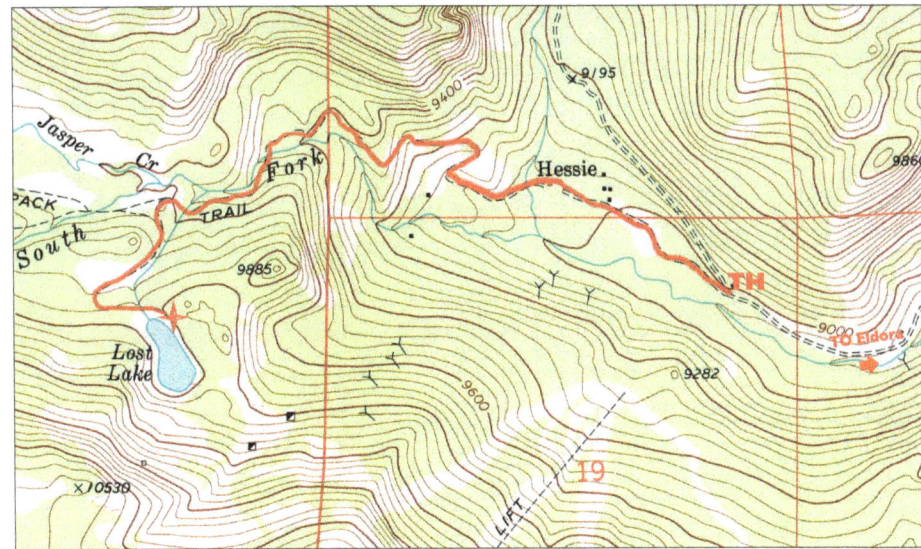

The trail today

The best way to access the popular trail to Lost Lake is to ride Boulder County's shuttle bus from the RTD parking lot in Nederland to the trailhead. The free shuttle operates on weekends and holidays from June through September and runs every 15 or 20 minutes. If you drive to the trailhead, be aware that only designated parking is available along the Fourth of July Road (CR 111). Parking is only allowed between signs. Violators will be fined $50 or towed.

The moderate hike starts on a boardwalk alongside the creek and then climbs 800 feet in 1.5 miles on the old road that has served as a connection between Eldora and Lost Lake for over a century. The road passes a couple of waterfalls and through aspen groves that are stunning in the fall. You can continue your hike up behind the lake to the remains of the old mines.

The lake is a perfect spot to stop for lunch, let the kids watch the fish jump, and take in the spectacular scenery.

CHAUTAUQUA

THEN AND NOW—A group of Rocky Mountain Climbers Club hikers paused for a photo on Flagstaff Road in 1916. Today, the dirt road that was hiked as much as driven in the early 1900s is a paved road used by vehicles and bikes.

Boulder's mountain playground

The East Coast Chautauqua movement arrived in Boulder when a group of Texas educators decided that the new city of Boulder would be a good spot for an educational mountain retreat and a way to escape the summer heat in their home state.

Boulder's Chautauqua opened on July 4, 1898, at "Texado Park" and quickly grew into a popular destination for individuals and families to

THEN AND NOW
Four members of the Chautauqua Pedestrian Club posed on top of Tomato Rock on July 30, 1902. Edwin Chamberlain, the man in the black cap, is credited with naming Royal Arch and Alamo Rock. Chamberlain was an ardent Mason, studying for his Royal Arch degree. One morning while hiking, his companion looked up at the distinctive rock formation and said, "Edwin, there is your Royal Arch." Below is Tomato Rock today.

A group of RMCC climbers posed at Royal Arch in 1916.

spend the summer attending lectures and musical performances, and participating in mountain outings. "Recreation will be combined with the Assembly feature, and excursions into the mountains will receive the attention which such health giving exercise deserves," claimed the Chautauquan magazine.

Boulder's Chautauqua was uniquely qualified to provide quick access for tramping in the adjacent foothills, and climbing (all hiking in the 1800s was called climbing) enthusiasts organized the Chautauqua Pedestrian Club in 1902. Four years later it was replaced by the Colorado Chautauqua Climbers Club. Few trails existed, and members found safety and companionship in the club, which organized guided hikes for both newcomers and seasoned climbers.

Fueled by a ravenous appetite for mountain adventures, early guides started building trails that were accessible to almost everyone. Chautauqua's "official" photographer Joseph B. Sturtevant (better known as Rocky Mountain Joe) and residents of Chautauqua constructed the Bluebell Canyon Trail in 1900, and after that they built a trail to Royal Arch.

Sturtevant was one of Boulder's more colorful characters around the turn of the century. In addition to his photography, Rocky Mountain Joe operated a burro train that gave students and tourists rides in the hills around Boulder.

THEN
These Chautauquans stopped "near Chautauqua Spring No. 6" for a photograph by Rocky Mountain Joe.

NOW
Today's Bluebell Spur Trail hasn't changed much.

Climbers who camped out on Flagstaff Mountain woke to a glorious sunrise on July 31, 1912.

The Colorado Chautauqua Climbers Club changed its name in 1908 to Rocky Mountain Climbers Club to include a wider range of members, and its numbers kept growing, along with the number of club-sponsored excursions.

The club organized outings that catered to different abilities, with graduated difficulties to encourage sea level to tundra acclimatization as quickly and painlessly as possible. Climbs were graded with a system of five "degrees" from easy nearby objectives to several-days-long, high-mountain trips. Climbing to Royal Arch earned a third degree, and fifth degrees were awarded to members who climbed to 14,000 feet. Steak fries at the end of increasingly difficult climbs were followed by introductory overnight hikes to the top of Flagstaff Mountain. Members who attended the steak fry campfires and participated in the songs, skits, stories, and jokes became lifelong friends.

The first overnight adventure for new members was to Flagstaff Mountain. It started with an evening at the Chautauqua Auditorium, and then the group took plenty of wraps and blankets to the top of the mountain. The next morning "every climber arose at 4:30 to see a…wonderful sunrise…It was as if the whole plain were a seething sea before the glorious sun covering the plains, hemmed in on the west and north by rocky reefs and cliffs," reported the R.M.C.C. Bulletin.

Above: A steak fry on a Four Mile hike in 1921. Below: Climbers who spent the night on top of Flagstaff Mountain prepared for their descent back to town on July 31, 1912.

A room designed for the RMCC was included on the lower floor of the Community House when it was built on the Chautauqua grounds in 1916 and 1917. Climbers Club members contributed a significant amount of money for the project, and members donated labor, including collecting stone for the rock walls of the building's lower level. Before long, the RMCC room was "the most popular place in Boulder," according to a Boulder newspaper.

RMCC guides and members began marking the trails in the Chautauqua area in 1924, often using old stone quarry and log skid roads, but the major push for blazing and constructing trails was made by the Civilian Conservation Corps in the '30s. The CCC was one of the New Deal programs created by President Franklin D. Roosevelt to fight the Great Depression. It was designed to put thousands of unemployed young men to work on public projects and operated from 1933 to 1942.

These two hikers showed off recommended climbing gear.

During those same years the Rocky Mountain Climbers Club held overnight working parties to improve the conditions of the trails, and Boulder's trail system flourished.

Ma and Pa Greenman

Ernest "Dad" Greenman and his wife, Ermin or "Mattie," joined the Rocky Mountain Climbers Club in 1913. Dad Greenman was associated with his brother in the Greenman Drug and Stationery Store on Pearl Street in Boulder and managed their branch store on University Hill until 1945, but he and his wife are most well known for their association with RMCC.

Dad Greenman first climbed the Third Flatiron in 1912, and made his last and 101st ascent in 1940. He led scores of university students and others to the top of what he affectionately called "The Big Rock."

He recorded his trips to the top of the Third Flatiron in a small leather-covered pocket notebook. His note about his first climb on July 14, 1912, said: "A recently healed broken arm proved somewhat of a handicap. Climbed on to Green, Kossler's Lake and Flagstaff Mt." Other entries record the retrieval of fallen climbers, and experiences with students. On Trip Number 26 in May of 1929, Greenman and another climber left a new register in the iron tube that the University of Colorado Hikers Club had placed there in 1922. Time

Dad Greenman (above), Fred Fair, Ralph Squires, and Paul Blanchard guided a trip over Arapaho Pass in 1927. Baker Armstrong, who was 16 at the time, remembered they went across the Divide from Brainard Lake to Monarch Lake. They camped that night, and the next day they went over Arapaho Pass and back to the cars. "Everyone was pretty tired, it was a pretty long trip," remembered Armstrong. "Dad Greenman didn't stop to get into the cars. He just walked the rest of the way into Eldora."

Above: Ma Greenman posed with a group of climbers. She's on the left corner of the roof of the cabin. The woman and children on the right side of the roof are showing off their hobnail boots. Below: Pa and Ma Greenman posed for a photographer during an RMCC hike to Arapaho Pass in 1920.

Hikers stopped at one of the springs built and maintained by RMCC members on the Chautauqua trails. Local plumbers donated the pipe necessary to keep the various springs flowing, and Dad Greenman often repaired the springs, which were subject to vandalism as well as normal wear and tear. Springs eliminated the need to carry a thermos on hikes in the Chautauqua area.

up: "14½ minutes." Other climbs weren't as fast, some ending at 1 or 2 in the morning after helping "tenderfeet" down from the summit using a rope. He was never paid for guiding people, and he and his wife led hundreds of hikers to Arapaho Glacier, Long's Peak, Jasper Lake, James Peak, and other popular destinations.

On his shorter trips Dad Greenman took time to develop springs, improve trails, and scatter flower and tree seeds, whose progeny are still growing in Boulder and the canyons west of the city. He organized many trail-building and trail-marking expeditions, and posted warning signs about fires and flower picking. He helped fight forest fires, and was frequently called to rescue Flatirons climbers who found themselves in trouble. When there were no organized mountaineering schools or rescue teams, Dad Greenman was known as the "One Man Rescue Group." The year before he died at the age of 82 he could be seen, usually alone, heading for the mountains with his shovel or hoe to do some work on the trails, including his namesake trail: the E.M. Greenman Trail.

The Chautauqua ski hill

Skiing was an infant sport when Boulder decided to build a ski area in its backyard. Workers removed boulders, raked, and seeded the slopes of Chautauqua Park to create the Chautauqua Mesa ski area. A 200-foot rope tow was installed, powered by a Dodge gasoline engine from a World War II Army truck. The area opened for the 1947-48 season under the direction of University of Colorado ski coach Steve Bradley.

The next season the top of the lift was moved 850 feet uphill. Entrepreneur Harris "Tommy" Thompson cleared boulders to make way for the 850-foot ski tow on the west end of Chautauqua Meadow. Lights were installed for night skiing, and field telephones connected lift operators at the top and bottom of the rope tow.

Lift tickets were $1 for adults and 50 cents for children under 12. Lessons were free. Most skiers bought used equipment left

over from the U.S. Army's 10th Mountain Division which had trained at Camp Hale in Colorado.

A beginners' jump, for distances of 15 to 40 feet, was built of dirt and snow. For the 1949 season two more jumps were added for intermediate and advanced skiers.

Unfortunately, the next few winters were warm, and vandals cut the rope tow rope. The ski area didn't open again until 1962, this time with volunteer lift operators, and lift tickets were free. Vandalism and poor snow conditions the next year again closed the ski area, and it never reopened.

Today the contours of the ski jumps between Chautauqua Mesa and Gregory Canyon are still visible, and sledders benefit from all the rock clearing and seeding done by hopeful skiers in the 1940s.

Above left: A lift operator helped a young skier use the rope tow. The 200-foot tow was located south of Sixth Street and Baseline Road. Above right: Boulder youth received ski lessons from Ed Kirst. The lessons were given on Chautauqua Hill through the city recreation program.

Opposite page: Spectators watched as Steve Bradley performed on the ski jump during the opening of Chautauqua Mesa Ski Area.

Rocky Mountain Joe

When the Boulder Chautauqua opened in 1898, Rocky Mountain Joe Sturtevant was named its official photographer.

By that time, Sturtevant was already a well-known character in Boulder both for the tall tales he told about his time as an Indian scout and for his distinctive long hair, goatee, and Wild West buckskins.

He moved to Boulder sometime around 1876 and worked as an artist, painting houses, hanging wallpaper, and lettering signs. Then he opened the first of several photography studios and carried his five-by-seven glass plate camera everywhere, often traveling up Boulder Canyon with pioneer stage and tallyho driver Mart Parsons to take photos of their trip, which he could then sell to the passengers.

Sturtevant built a photography studio on the Chautauqua grounds called The Woodbine where visitors could have their portrait taken for 25 cents, and he often led excursions into the mountains above Chautauqua. He became one of Boulder's most prolific photographers. His images, which are now in libraries and museums, chronicle the development of the new city of Boulder and the trails into the mountains from Chautauqua.

After Sturtevant died in 1910, his friend Mart Parsons salvaged 3,500 glass plates from his home and put his own initials, MRP, on them, including ones that were not taken by Sturtevant. Parsons later bequeathed all the glass plates to the Boulder Historical Society.

Ed Tangen

Ed Tangen left us with this self-portrait.

Edwin Tangen came to the U.S. from Norway when he was a child and moved to Boulder from Chicago in 1900. He was a lifelong bachelor who often accompanied Rocky Mountain Climbers Club members on their tramps in the mountains. Known as The Pictureman, he took many of the photographs in this book.

In addition to his photos from mountain trips, Tangen was well known for the revolutionary methods he introduced into criminal investigation. He took microphotographs that could link a specific bullet to a specific gun, and he compiled and photographed an extensive collection of bullets. He then cataloged and cross-indexed them as to type of rifling, make of gun, and caliber of ammunition. Tangen served as the identification officer for the Boulder County Sheriff's Office from 1923 to 1951. He often traveled to nearby states to testify in court cases.

Tangen first signed his photos with a T. His signature later became a T enclosed in a diamond, like the one in the lower right of this photo he took of a hike with RMCC to Needle's Eye above Chautauqua in 1913.

Baker Armstrong: climber and magician

When Baker Armstrong was 12 years old he went with Rocky Mountain Climbers Club to Kossler Reservoir, a four-mile hike from Boulder. He also climbed Arapaho Peak that year. When he was 14, he made most of the club's climbs, including Longs Peak. When Armstrong was 17 his father built a cabin at Brainard Lake, and when he was 20, Mr. C.C. Thorsten, who owned Camp Audubon, across the lake, wanted him to run his mountain climbing program. He did that from 1928 to 1937. He also worked for the Houston Chamber of Commerce, owned a business in Texas, and worked at the Audubon Boys' Camp and for Rocky Mountain Rescue Group.

But what many people remembered most about Baker was his magic show at Chautauqua during two seasons, 1928 and 1930. As Rekab the Wizard (Rekab is Baker spelled backwards), Baker presented an evening of entertainment and sleight of hand that promised to "dazzle the eyes of young and old." His most famous trick was to escape from a tightly locked and roped box.

READY TO GO—Baker Armstrong and friends are packed and ready for their trip to Longs Peak with the RMCC in 1924. Left: Rekab the Wizard performed at Chautauqua.

THEN AND NOW Chautauqua Auditorium, the starting point of many RMCC hikes and where Baker Armstrong performed as Rekab, still stands proudly under the Flatirons.

One of the Rocky Mountain Climbers Club hikes to Split Rock in 1920 attracted a lot of participants.

The King's Gate entrance to Chautauqua from Baseline Road was featured on this hand-colored postcard.

The view from Woods Quarry is as spectacular today as it was when RMCC climbers trekked there.

Ralph Squires and Ma Greenman guided many of the Rocky Mountain Climbers Club hikes.

Top: Long skirts made climbing rocks in the hills above Chautauqua difficult, but not impossible with a little help from friends. Bottom: Hiking apparel has changed over the years, but Woods Quarry is still a whimsical spot to hang out with friends. Woods Quarry began operation in the late 1890s and was owned by Frank Wood and Jonas Bergheim. Sandstone from the quarry was used throughout Boulder for sidewalks and buildings. Because of the difficult access it did not last long and was purchased by the City of Boulder in 1920 for conservation and recreation.

Museums/Side Trips

★ Chautauqua Dining Hall (historical photos on walls)

★ Cottage #100 (now general store and ice cream)

★ Tours: www.chautauqua.com (mobile phone interpretive audio tour available, 303-952-1600; guided tours available late May through October)

Hike to Woods Quarry

Trail maps are available at the Chautauqua Ranger Cottage. Just west of the Auditorium is the Academic Hall, where you can get a map of the historic phone tour of Chautauqua. To learn about the site you're looking at, dial 303-952-1600 and enter the # for the site.

From the Ranger Cottage hike up Bluebell Road 0.3 miles to the intersection with the Mesa Trail. Head south on the Mesa Trail 0.5 miles to the well-marked trail to Woods Quarry. Woods Quarry is a 0.4-mile loop. If you come from the north it is a moderate uphill climb. The south access is steeper. At the south end of the loop where it meets the Mesa Trail is the historic Roosa Cabin. Woods Quarry has a wonderful view of the plains and is a great place to relax and enjoy a snack.

Returning from Woods Quarry you can take the Enchanted Mesa Trail (gentle) or McClintock Trail (steep) to return to the Chautauqua Auditorium.

The historic Roosa Cabin

Acknowledgements

This book wouldn't have been possible without a lot of help, and we have many people to thank. First on our list is the Rocky Mountain Climbers Club and its president Peter Arts. The club gernerously opened their doors to us and shared their history, which in many ways became the foundation of the book. Edie DeWeese and Bruce Baker were likewise open with the history of the Rock Creek ski area, as was Nancy Billings Colton with her scrapbooks and memories of her grandfather Nort Billings. Tim Nicklas spent a great deal of time with us as we pored over photos and ephemera in the Grand County Historical Association's museum in Hot Sulphur Springs.

For their inestimable help with our research, thanks go to Rocky Mountain National Park Archivist Kelly Cahill, Carnegie Branch Library Manager Wendy Hall, Chautauqua historian and archivist Kate Gerard, Estes Park Museum Curator of Collections Naomi Gerakios Mucci, Denver Public Library's Coi Drummond-Gehrig, and historian Carol Taylor.

Many thanks also go to Bobbie Heisterkamp, Mike Shaw, Suzanne Silverthorn, Janet Roberston, Bill Briggs, and Caroline Schmiedt who searched their collections of postcards and photos and shared what they found with us.

We also want to express our gratitude to our perceptive and supportive editors Mary Jarrett and Bill Ikler for all their invaluable editorial insights and proofreading.

Many other people, too numerous to name, helped us along the way, and we thank you all—your help was invaluable.

We hope today's readers will enjoy this peek at the past as much as we have.

Photo credits

Cover photos: courtesy Rocky Mountain Climbers Club
iv: courtesy Rocky Mountain Climbers Club
1: Grand County Museum, Hot Sulphur Springs
2: photo by Kay Turnbaugh
3: (top) Rocky Mountain National Park; (bottom) photo by Kay Turnbaugh
4: Rocky Mountain National Park
5: (both) Grand County Museum, Hot Sulphur Springs
6-7: Estes Park Museum
8: (left) postcard of F.P. Clatworthy photo is courtesy Caroline Schmiedt; (right) Grand County Museum, Hot Sulphur Springs
9: (left) Bobbie Heisterkamp collection; (right) photo by Kay Turnbaugh
10: Library of Congress
11: Wikimedia photo by McCormack
12-13: Rocky Mountain National Park
14: Bobbie Heisterkamp collection
16: photo by Kay Turnbaugh
17-26: historic photos courtesy Bruce Baker and Edie DeWeese, today photos by Kay Turnbaugh
27: Carnegie Branch Library for Local History, Allenspark photograph collection
28: (both) courtesy Bruce Baker
29: Colorado Ski Hall of Fame
30: courtesy Nancy Billings Colton
31: Estes Park Museum
32: courtesy Nancy Billings Colton
33: photo by Kay Turnbaugh
34: historic map courtesy Tillotson family
35: Library of Congress
36: photo by Kay Turnbaugh
37: Carnegie Library for Local History/Museum of Boulder Collection
40-41: Carnegie Library for Local History/Museum of Boulder Collection
43: Carnegie Library for Local History/Museum of Boulder Collection
44: photo by Kay Turnbaugh
45: Carnegie Library for Local History/Museum of Boulder Collection
46: (top) courtesy Rocky Mountain Climbers Club; (bottom) Carnegie Library for Local History/Museum of Boulder Collection
47: (top) Carnegie Library for Local History/Museum of Boulder Collection; (bottom) photo by Kay Turnbaugh
48: (top) photo by Kay Turnbaugh; (bottom) Carnegie Library for Local History/Museum of Boulder Collection
49: photo by Kay Turnbaugh
51: courtesy Rocky Mountain Climbers Club
52: photo by Kay Turnbaugh
53: Eben Fine, courtesy Rocky Mountain Climbers Club; Fred Fair, Carnegie Library for Local History
54: courtesy Rocky Mountain Climbers Club
55: Carnegie Library for Local History/Museum of Boulder Collection
57: courtesy Rocky Mountain Climbers Club
59: courtesy Rocky Mountain Climbers Club
60: photo by Kay Turnbaugh
61: (top) courtesy Rocky Mountain Climbers Club; (bottom) photo by Kay Turnbaugh
62-64: courtesy Rocky Mountain Climbers Club
65: photo by Kay Turnbaugh
66: courtesy Rocky Mountain Climbers Club
68: photo by Kay Turnbaugh
69: courtesy Rocky Mountain Climbers Club
70: photo by Kay Turnbaugh
71: Grand County Museum, Hot Sulphur Springs
72: Denver Public Library, Western History Collection, #27
71-72: (bottom) Library of Congress
73: Leda Reed
74: Grand County Museum, Hot Sulphur Springs
76: (top) Denver Public Library, Western History Collection, X-7383; (bottom) Grand County Museum, Hot Sulphur Springs
77: (top) courtesy Rocky Mountain Climbers Club; (bottom) photo by Kay Turnbaugh
78: (top) Grand County Museum, Hot Sulphur Springs; (bottom) photo by Kay Turnbaugh
79: (top) Grand County Museum, Hot Sulphur Springs; (bottom left) courtesy Turnbaugh family, (bottom right) Wikipedia
80: Marjorie Perry, courtesy Lee Tillotson; Elinor Kingery, courtesy Hugh Kingery
81: Grand County Museum, Hot Sulphur Springs
82: Denver Public Library, Western History Collection, Z-1031
83: (top) Grand County Museum, Hot Sulphur Springs; (bottom) photo by Kay Turnbaugh
84: (top) Grand County Museum, Hot Sulphur Springs; (bottom) Denver Public Library, Western History Collection, F-45143
85: (right) Grand County Museum, Hot Sulphur Springs
86: (top) Grand County Museum, Hot Sulphur Springs; (bottom) courtesy Mike Shaw
88: photo by Kay Turnbaugh
91: Carnegie Library for Local History/Museum of Boulder Collection

92: photo by Kay Turnbaugh
93-94: Carnegie Library for Local History/Museum of Boulder Collection
95: (top) Eldora Community/Bolton Collection ; (bottom) photo by Kay Turnbaugh
96: (top) Carnegie Library for Local History/Museum of Boulder Collection (bottom) Carnegie Library for Local History
97: (top) Carnegie Library for Local History/Museum of Boulder Collection; (bottom) photo by Lee Tillotson
98: Carnegie Library for Local History/Museum of Boulder Collection
100-101: Carnegie Library for Local History/Museum of Boulder Collection
102: (top) Denver Public Library, Western History Collection, L-338; (bottom) photo by Kay Turnbaugh
103: (top) Carnegie Library for Local History/Museum of Boulder Collection; (bottom) courtesy Kay Turnbaugh
104: (top) Carnegie Library for Local History/Museum of Boulder Collection; (bottom) USGS
105: photo by Lee Tillotson
107: courtesy Rocky Mountain Climbers Club
108: photo by Kay Turnbaugh
109: Eldora Community/Bolton Collection
110-111: photo by Kay Turnbaugh
112-113: (top) Barbara Lawlor; (bottom) Eldora Community/Bolton Collection
114: photo by Kay Turnbaugh
115-116: Eldora Community/Bolton Collection
117: photos by Kay Turnbaugh
119: courtesy Rocky Mountain Climbers Club
120: photo by Lee Tillotson
121: (top) Carnegie Library for Local History; (bottom) photo by Lee Tillotson
122: courtesy Rocky Mountain Climbers Club
123: Carnegie Library for Local History/Museum of Boulder Collection
124: photo by Lee Tillotson
125-130 courtesy Rocky Mountain Climbers Club
131-133: Carnegie Library for Local History/Museum of Boulder Collection
134-135: Courtesy Rocky Mountain Climbers Club
136: (top) Mike Shaw; (bottom) photo by Kay Turnbaugh
137-138: (large map) courtesy Colorado Chautauqua Association, artist unknown; (bottom photos, left to right), courtesy Rocky Mountain Climbers Club, courtesy Mike Shaw, photo by Lee Tillotson, courtesy Rocky Mountain Climbers Club
139: (top) Carnegie Library for Local History/Museum of Boulder Collection; (bottom) photo by Lee Tillotson
140: photo by Lee Tillotson

Map credits

All current-day maps are based on United States Geological Survey (USGS) maps and routes added by the authors, with these exceptions:

Overview Map: Colorado Department of Transportation map with routes added
140: courtesy City of Boulder Open Space and Mountain Parks, with route added by the authors.

All historic maps are from the USGS with these exceptions:

15: historic map from pamphlet: *Mountaineering in the Rocky Mountain National Park*, compiled by Roger W. Toll, from the Records of the Colorado Mountain Club, published 1921 by Department of the Interior
34: historic 1948 USGS map, "Denver Mountain Area," courtesy Tillotson family
67: historic map courtesy Colorado Chautauqua Association
118: detail of Henry R. Drumm Pocket Map of Boulder County, published in 1932, courtesy Kay Turnbaugh

Bibliography

Arps, Louisa Ward, and Kingery, Elinor Eppich, *High Country Names, Rocky Mountain National Park and Indian Peaks*. Boulder, Colorado: Johnson Books, 1977, 1994.

Becker, Isabel M., *Nederland: A Trip to Cloudland*. Denver, Colorado: Scott Becker Press, 1989.

Benedict, James B., *Arapaho Pass: Glacial Geology and Archeology at the Crest of the Colorado Front Range*. Boulder, Colorado: D & K Printing, 1985.

Bollinger, Edward T., *Rails That Climb, The Story of the Moffat Road*. Santa Fe, New Mexico: The Rydal Press, 1950.

Boyd, Leanne C., and Carson, H. Glenn, *Atlas of Colorado Ghost Towns*, Volume 1. Deming, New Mexico: Cache Press, 1984.

Bronski, Peter, *Powder Ghost Towns, Epic Backcountry Runs in Colorado's Lost Ski Resorts*. Birmingham, Alabama: Wilderness Press, 2008.

Brown, Robert L., *Ghost Towns of the Colorado Rockies*. Caldwell, Idaho: The Caxton Printers, Ltd., 1969.

Buchanan, John W., and Doris G. Buchanan, *The Story of Ghost Town Caribou*. Boulder, Colorado: Boulder Publishing, Inc., 1957.

Buchholtz, C.W., *Rocky Mountain National Park: A History*. Niwot, Colorado: University Press of Colorado, 1983.

Cobb, Harrison S., *Prospecting Our Past: Gold, Silver and Tungsten Mills of Boulder County*. Longmont, Colorado: The Book Lode, 1999

Corona Telegraph, Issue #33 (Vol. 13, No. 2), February, 2016.

Corona Telegraph, Issue #34 (Vol. 14, No. 1), November, 2016.

Corona Telegraph, Issue #35 (Vol. 14, No. 2), April, 2017.

Cornell, Virginia, *Doc Susie, The True Story of a Country Physician in the Colorado Rockies*. Carpinteria California: Manifest Publications, 1991.

Crossen, Forest, *The Switzerland Trail of America*. Fort Collins, Colorado: Robinson Press, 1978.

Crossen, Forest, *Western Yesterdays, Vol. 1*. Boulder, Colorado: Boulder Publishing Company, 1965.

Crossen, Forest, *Western Yesterdays, Vol. X, David Moffat's Hill Men*. Fort Collins, Colorado: Robinson Press, 1976.

Crifasi, Robert R., *A Land Made from Water, Appropriation and the Evolution of Colorado's Landscape, Ditches, and Water Institutions*. Boulder, Colorado: University Press of Colorado, 2015.

Cushman, Ruth Carol, and Glenn Cushman, *Boulder Hiking Trails, Fourth Edition*. Boulder, Colorado: Pruett Publishing Company, 2006.

Cushman, Ruth Carol, and Stephen R. Jones, "September Nature Almanac: Apples Gone Wild in Boulder Foothills," *www.dailycamera.com,* updated August 29, 2016.

Dallas, Sandra, *No More than Five in a Bed, Colorado Hotels in the Old Days*. Norman, Oklahoma: University of Oklahoma Press, 1967.

Follansbee, Robert, and Leon R. Sawyer, *Floods in Colorado, United States Department of the Interior, Geological Survey Water-Supply Paper 997*. Washington: U.S. Government Printing Office, 1948.

Galey, Mary, *The Grand Assembly, the Story of Life at the Colorado Chautauqua, Third Edition*. Boulder, Colorado: Colorado Chautauqua Association, 2015.

Griswold, P.R., *Before the Moffat Tunnel, Celebrating the Centennial Arrival of the First Train to Tolland*. Brighton, Colorado: Sherm Conners Publishing, 2004.

Griswold, P.R., *David Moffat's Denver Northwestern and Pacific*. Denver, Colorado: Rocky Mountain Railroad Club, 1995.

Hafnor, John, *Strange But True, Colorado: Weird Tales of the Wild West*. Fort Collins, Colorado: Long Pine Productions, 2005.

Huber, Thomas P., *Colorado Byways, A Guide Through Scenic and Historic Landscapes*. Boulder, Colorado: University of Colorado Press, 1997.

Kemp, Donald C., and Langley, John R., *Happy Valley, A Promoter's Paradise*. Denver, Colorado: Smith-Brooks Printing Co., 1945.

Kemp, Donald C., *Silver, Gold and Black Iron, A Story of the Grand Island Mining District of Boulder County, Colorado*. Denver, Colorado: Sage Books, 1960.

Knowlton, Lorna, second edition edited by Edie DeWeese, *Weaving Mountain Memories, Recollections of the Allenspark Area*. Allenspark, Colorado: Allenspark Wind, 2011.

Lambrecht, Mona, and Boulder History Museum, *Boulder 1859-1919*. Charleston, South Carolina: Arcadia Publishing.

Meier, Thomas J., *Ed Tangen, The Pictureman, A Photographic History of the Boulder Region, Early Twentieth Century*. Boulder, Colorado: Boulder Creek Press, 1994.

Pettem, Silvia, *Excursions from Peak to Peak Then and Now*. Longmont, Colorado: The Book Lode, 1997.

Pettem Silvia, *Guide to Historic Western Boulder County*. Evergreen, Colorado: Cordillera Press, 1989.

Reilly-McNellan, Mary, Lise Cook Cordsen, Judith Gould Dayhoff, and Barbara Walsh Myers, *If These Stones Could Talk, Tales from Columbia Cemetery, Boulder, Colorado*. Boulder Colorado: Johnson Books, 2012.

Robertson, Janet, *The Magnificent Mountain Women: Adventures in the Colorado Rockies*. Lincoln, Nebraska and London: University of Nebraksa Press, 1990

Robertson, Janet, "Tracks on Tracks," skiinghistory.org, September-October 2013, web.

Rollins Pass Restoration Association, *The Moffat Road, A Self-Guiding Auto Tour*. Longmont, Colorado: Rollins Pass Restoration Association (reprint by), 1996.

Sherard, Gerald E., "A Short History of the Colorado State Penitentiary," *https://www.colorado.gov*, Colorado State Archives.

Silverthorn, Suzanne, *Rocky Mountain Tour, Estes Park, Rocky Mountain National Park, & Grand Lake*. Atglen, Pennsylvania: Schiffer Publishing Ltd., 2008.

Smith, Duane A., Silver Saga, the Story of Caribou, Colorado, Revised Edition. Boulder, Colorado: University Press of Colorado, 2003.

Smith, Phyllis, *A History of Boulder's Transportation, 1858 - 1984*. Boulder, Colorado, prepared for the Transportation Division, City of Boulder, March 1984.

Stone, Wilbur Fiske (editor), *History of Colorado, Volume 4*, Chicago: S.J. Clarke, 1918.

Toll, Roger, *Mountaineering in the Rocky Mountain National Park*, Washington: Government Print Office, 1921.

Turnbaugh, Kay, and Lee Tillotson, *Rocky Mountain National Park Dining Room Girl: The Summer of 1926 at the Horseshoe Inn*. Nederland, Colorado: Perigo Press, 2015.

Wright, B. Travis, MPS, and Kate Wright, MBA, *Rollins Pass*. Charleston, South Carolina: Arcadia Publishing, 2018.

Personal interviews with the authors:

Bruce Baker, with Lee Tillotson, January 13, 2018, Longmont, Colorado.

Nancy Billings Colton, with Lee Tillotson and Kay Turnbaugh, September 15, 2015, Nederland, Colorado.

Edie DeWeese, with Lee Tillotson and Kay Turnbaugh, July 21, 2017, Allenspark, Colorado.

Tim Nicklas, with Lee Tillotson and Kay Turnbaugh, August 9, 2017, Grand County Museum, Hot Sulphur Springs, Colorado.

Index

Allenspark 18–34
Allenspark Ski Club 22
Alpine Visitors Center 13, 16
Alvord, C.C. 60
Andrews, D.M. 52
Arapaho Glacier 52, 53, 54, 55, 56, 57, 58, 60, 61, 68
Arapaho Glacier Trail 60, 68
Arapaho Pass 52–68, 128, 129
Arapaho Peak 94, 101
Armstrong, Baker 128, 135, 136

Baker, Bruce 23
Baker, Clint 22, 23, 26
Baker, Philip 25
Barker Dam 46
Benedict, Jim 65
Bernard, T.H. 99–101
Billings, Nort 21, 22, 30, 31, 32
Blanchard, Paul 128
Bluebell Canyon Trail 122
Bluebell Spur Trail 124
Boulder Canyon 39
Boulder Chamber of Commerce 54, 56, 58
Boulder Wagon Trail 88
Bradley, Steve 131
Brainard Lake 128, 135

Camp Francis 46
Camp Hale 21, 132
Caribou 60, 62, 91–106
Caribou Brass Band 103
Caribou school 99–101
Central City 93, 94, 96, 100, 103, 109
Chamberlain, Edwin 121
Chasm Falls 7
Chautauqua 38, 119–140
Chautauqua Auditorium 126, 136, 140
Chautauqua Mesa ski area 131–132
Chautauqua Pedestrian Club 121, 122

Chautauqua Ranger Cottage 140
Civilian Conservation Corps 127
Colorado Chautauqua Climbers Club 122
Colorado Mountain Club 57
Colorado & Northwestern Railroad 37, 38, 39, 40, 43, 45
Colorado Railroad Museum 45, 49
Colorado Ski Hall of Fame 29, 32
Colorado Snowsports Museum and Hall of Fame 29
Colorado State Penitentiary 4, 10
Corona 69–90
Cunningham, Gerry and Ann 26

Davis, Captain J.H. 115
Davis, Wilson 116
Denver and Salt Lake Western Railroad Company 14
Denver, Boulder, & Western Railroad 39
Denver, Northeastern & Pacific Railway 72
Denver & Salt Lake Railroad 82
Dog's Trail 2

East Portal of the Moffat Tunnel 88
Eldora 39, 46, 58, 60, 68, 108, 110, 111, 113, 115, 118
Enchanted Mesa Trail 140
Engine 30 41, 45, 49
Eppich, Elinor 80–82

Fair, Fred 53, 55, 56, 128
Fall River Canyon 4
Fall River Pass 4
Fall River Road 2–16
Fine, Eben G. 53
Flagstaff Road 120
Forest Canyon Pass 3
Forest Canyon Trail 3

Fourmile Canyon (Four Mile Cañon) 38, 42
Fourth of July campground 58
Fourth of July Mine 60, 63, 64, 65
Fourth of July Trailhead 68
Frankeberger, Jason Lee 43
Frankeberger, Minette 43

Giant's Ladder 75, 82, 86
Glacier Lake 36, 39
Glacier Route 51, 57, 67
Gold Hill 38, 49
Grant, President Ulysses S. 93, 103
Greenman, Ermin "Ma" 128–130, 138
Greenman, Ernest "Dad" or "Pa" 46, 47, 128–130
Gregory Canyon 132

Hansen, Hans 20
Harsh, Jim 30, 31
Haugen, Anders 29
Haugen, Lars 20, 21, 27, 29, 80
Haugen Slide 20, 21, 27, 28, 29
Hessie 111, 115–116
Hill Route 70, 75, 80
Hottel, Bill 21
Howelsen, Carl 20
Hurt, George 21

Indian Peaks Wilderness 58

James Peak Wilderness 88
Jelsema, Ted 31
Jenny Lake 72, 74, 82

Kemp, Donald C. 60
Kingery, Elinor 80–82

Lake Placid Olympics 32
Langley, John R. 62

Longs Peak 36, 38
Lost Lake 107–118
Lytle, George 96

Matlack, Anne 27
Maxwell, James P. 55
McClintock Trail 140
McQueary, Dick 7
Mills, Enos 53, 57
Milner Pass 9, 14, 16
Milner, T.J. 14
Moffat, David 72
Moffat Road 72, 73, 74, 75, 76, 80, 85, 88
Monarch Lake 128
Mont Alto 35–50

Needle's Eye Tunnel 72, 85, 86, 88
New Jersey Mill 97, 105, 106
Norway Mill 110

Orear, G.W. 115–116

Paddock, Laurence 58
Parsons, Mart 133
Peak to Peak Scenic Byway 49
Perry, Marjorie 80–82
Point Frankeberger 43
Potosi Mining Company 102
Poudre Lake 2
Poudre Lake spires 9
Pumphouse Lake 89–90

Rainbow Lakes 55, 56, 57, 58
Rekab the Wizard 135
Revenge Mine 109, 113
Rock Creek Ski Area 17–34
Rocky Mountain Climbers Club 46, 52, 54, 57, 59, 61, 62, 64, 66, 70, 77, 89, 108, 120–140

Rocky Mountain National Park 4, 53, 57, 58
Rocky Mountain National Park Ski Club 30, 31
Rollins Pass 69–90
Roosa Cabin 140
Royal Arch 121, 122, 126

Saint Vrain Mountain 25, 34
Saint Vrain Mountain Trailhead 34
Saint Vrain Ski Club 22
Schoolland, Dr. J.B. 45
Sherman House 95, 96, 98, 101
shuttle bus 118
ski courses or slides 28
Smith, Champ 115–116
snowshed 71, 72, 73, 77, 81, 84, 85, 86
South Arapaho Peak 53, 56, 57, 63
Split Rock 137
Squires, Ralph 128, 138
Steele, John 30, 31
Strawhum, F. M. 113
Sturtevant, Joseph B., a.k.a. Rocky Mountain Joe 122, 123, 133
Sunset 38, 39, 46
Switzerland Trail 35–50

Tangen, Edwin 134
Tenth Mountain Division 21, 132
Third Flatiron 128
Tolland 74, 75, 82, 86
Toll, Roger, Park Superintendent 13
Tomato Rock 121
Trail Ridge Road 2, 6, 53
Trowbridge, C.R. Acting Park Supervisor 7
Tynan, Thomas 6, 10

U.S. Gold Corporation 61
Ute Trail 4

Ward 20, 26, 29
Way, L.C., Park Superintendent 7
Wheeler, Herbert N. 52
Willow Creek 20, 21, 22, 27, 28
Woods Quarry 138, 139, 140

Yankee Doodle Lake 85, 88

About the authors

Kay Turnbaugh owned a weekly newspaper in Nederland, Colorado, for 27 years. She is the author of five other books: *Around Nederland*; the Willa Award-winning *The Last of the Wild West Cowgirls*; *Rocky Mountain National Park Dining Room Girl, The Summer of 1926 at the Horseshoe Inn* (with Lee Tillotson); *The Mountain Pine Beetle—Tiny but Mighty*; and co-author of the second edition of *Afoot & Afield: Denver, Boulder, Fort Collins, and Rocky Mountain National Park*.

Lee Tillotson is an avid outdoorswoman, and she and her husband were Student Conservation Association supervisors in several different National Parks, including Rocky Mountain National Park. She is a retired physical education teacher who also has taught cross-country skiing and led numerous historical hikes and snowshoe tours. She is co-author of *Rocky Mountain National Park Dining Room Girl, The Summer of 1926 at the Horseshoe Inn*.

www.ingramcontent.com/pod-product-compliance
Lightning Source LLC
Chambersburg PA
CBHW060926170426
43192CB00025B/2902